# Blessed And BROKEN

## The Mental Health Crisis In The Church

# Blessed And BROKEN

## The Mental Health Crisis In The Church

## Apostle Michael W. Moses

XULON PRESS

Xulon Press
2301 Lucien Way #415
Maitland, FL 32751
407.339.4217
www.xulonpress.com

Contribution by: Sonya T. Cruel, LCSW

Unless otherwise indicated, Scripture quotations taken from the Holy Bible, New International Version (NIV). Copyright © 1973, 1978, 1984, 2011 by Biblica, Inc.™. Used by permission. All rights reserved.

Scripture quotations taken from the New King James Version (NKJV). Copyright © 1982 by Thomas Nelson, Inc. Used by permission. All rights reserved.

Paperback ISBN-13: 978-1-66284-481-2
Ebook ISBN-13: 978-1-66284-482-9

# Table of Contents

# Foreword By:

**Sonya T. Cruel, LCSW**
**Transition Coach**
**www.sonyatcruel.com /**
**Sonya T. Cruel Consulting, LLC**

When we look at television and social media today, we see people with perfect lives. They have it all together. They are living their "best life." They are vacationing with friends, enjoying a girls' weekend trip to exotic all-inclusive resorts, or the guys getting together for weekend trips centered around their favorite sporting events. These images often lead us to believe that the happiness and joy that we see are genuine and real, but many times the reality is that they are **Blessed And Broken**!

In my profession, I regularly see people who are broken on the inside but look fabulous on the outside. Good people with unfinished business/traumas regarding their families, childhood, divorce, and many other life-altering events that have left them with incomplete transitions. This incompleteness continues to plague them both mentally and emotionally in their day-to-day adult lives. There is no way to heal from what we refuse to acknowledge or seek treatment for. People can bury, stuff, swallow, or even repress their issues so deep internally and pretend like there are no issues, but a trained eye can see it a mile away. It will come out in the way we speak, the choices that we make, how we relate to others and how we live our daily lives. Eventually the pressure of the pain can get so intense until they literally burst. Have you ever heard the saying, "pressure bursts pipes"? In the book *Blessed And Broken*, Apostle Moses not only shares the consequences of not dealing with unfinished business/traumas, but he has also done what few people are willing to do: he shares his most personal and private experiences. His vulnerability and transparency are a lesson for us all.

Apostle Moses starts out with a nail-on-the-head statement: "We can no longer afford to evaluate a leader's effectiveness by judging their giftedness, or outward appearance." Leaders are more than what we see when they stand before us on Sunday mornings. Some of us have a hard time understanding that leaders are people too, especially when there is a fall from grace. We forget leaders are just like us but with a different calling. They need support just like us "regular" believers do. His conversation on balance is so needed in ministry leadership today. He says, "There is never too much God, but there can be too much church." Some of us come from families where we attended church Sunday through Saturday, so being out of balance is a learned behavior.

We must ask ourselves: are we committed to Jesus or to man and his programs? I know of believers who have turned away from the church today because they were always in services growing up. I didn't say turned away from God but from church. So, what are we teaching our children about church and God? Do they have to be mutually exclusive?

This book not only tells real life stories for us to glean from, but also provides actual steps to take better care of our own mental and emotional health. He provides specific keys for maintaining good mental and emotional habits. He doesn't shy away from a need for a good mental health professional. I like to tell people, "Everyone needs Jesus and a good therapist." Notice I said *good*. I encourage people to look for a professional with which they can connect. This search can be frustrating sometimes, but don't give up if the first one is not a good fit. We must learn to see our mental and emotional health as being just as important as our physical health.

I would encourage everyone to take your time reading this book. Allow yourself to reflect on your own upbringing, your own life and ministry experiences that may have affected you in negative ways. Take that retrospective look inward and see where additional work is needed. Don't allow fear and shame to keep you from dealing with the broken areas of your life. This book, **Blessed and Broken**, is a great first step to wholeness.

# From the Author

As a church and a corporate business leader who has been personally affected by serious emotional and dissociative issues brought on by childhood traumas, I recognize the need for effective ministries inside the church that address its ever-increasing mental and emotional health concerns. This book was written to speak to the heart of the matter when it comes to mental and emotional health in the pulpit, as well as in the pews. This book was not designed to be preachy or too clinical, just real. You will find a few verbatim scripture quotes, and a few numerical scripture references. But my goal here is to lay aside the church stuff for a few moments and ask the question that many never get asked, or we do not care to answer truthfully:

*How are you really doing, my brothers and sisters?*

There is an unspoken rule in ministry for leaders, and that is: We do not talk about our weaknesses. We can talk about all the woes of ministry, but do we ever really talk about what's going on with us? For many years in ministry, I, like many believers, have suffered in silence when it comes to our mental and emotional health. So, in our journey together we will explore the parallel between those believers who have experienced parental/familial traumas vs. those who continually struggle with their mental and emotional health on into adulthood. It is my prayer that as you read this book, if you need to do so, you will find a path to your own mental and emotional healing and stability through mentorship, accountability, and professional help, if necessary. I also pray that you would find the courage to change "whatever" is necessary to get off the mental health roller coaster.

This book should serve as a wakeup call to the body of Christ. We must shed light on the needs of those in the body who struggle with mental and emotional issues.

We have relegated them to the outer court experience with God long enough. All believers, whether mentally stable all the time or not, should have a place where they know they are welcomed, loved, and understood.

I want you to know that even though we may struggle with issues of our own, it does not negate the "good works" we have been doing for Christ. Know that it is okay to be:

**"Blessed and Broken"**!

# Chapter 1

# Physician Heal Thyself

*If God Is Unable To Keep You, Then You Can't Be Kept*

One of the greatest and often undiscussed misconceptions about church leadership is that the person leading is "whole." Notice I didn't say qualified, because there are many qualified, dynamic, charismatic leaders who still may secretly struggle with mental or emotional issues. I, like many preachers, may have believed that when you go into ministry, and you are teaching the word and helping others to get healed, you yourself gets healed.

Now I'm not saying that God can't do it that way, but what do you do when He doesn't choose to do it that way? *We can no longer afford to evaluate a leader's effectiveness by judging their giftedness or outward appearance.* There are powerful and gifted leaders all over the body of Christ, but they still struggle with mental issues, emotional issues, childhood brokenness, and life-controlling issues.

What's interesting is that the signs are evident. More times than not, the ones closest to the individuals usually get to see the "breakdowns." From fits of rage to suicidal thoughts, bouts of depression, staying in bed for days on end but when Sunday morning comes, they are up and ready to go to church as if nothing ever happened. For many, this is a continual cycle, not just for preachers but for the people in the pews as well.

Those who know them best simply hope the individuals can maintain some sense of normalcy. They cover for and make excuses for the unusual behaviors. "But why?" you ask. "Why do they do it?" It is because they know all too well that if anyone found out, it could affect "The Ministry." In ministry, image is everything. Imagine the enormous pressure a husband/wife would be under to stand with their spouse, knowing they are struggling with infidelity, mental, and emotional issues.

Furthermore, these issues tend to affect their marriages. Spouses will routinely deal with many of the issues for a while, but often the offending partner does not choose to get help, and the marriages fail under the weight of the pressure.

I experienced my own bout with paranoid behaviors that nearly destroyed my marriage. My decisions were back and forth, all over the place. I was so fixated on the images I believed to be true, I could not focus on ministry. My sermon preparation suffered, my preaching suffered, and the ministry suffered. This only exacerbated the tension between my wife and me. Now I am sure there were people in the ministry who may have noticed something was going on with us, but I tried to hide it well. I would still preach on Sunday mornings and Thursday nights for Bible study, but I was a dry, empty shell. These things were my solace, so I was able to continue, but when the service was over, I was back to looking out for things to be wrong.

Drinking became one of my secret coping mechanisms if there is such a thing as a secret drinking habit. This in turn affected both my physical and spiritual man. So, I finally did what I should have done years earlier: I sought professional mental help. I started seeing a mental health specialist I found through my job's benefit program called "EAP" (Employee Assistance Program). I combined this with some good old-fashioned accountability to authority and saved my marriage, and of course I gained the healing that comes from giving one's issues to God.

During these sessions, getting someone else's objective view helped me to see myself and what I looked like to others: indecisive, crazy, and erratic. My professional helped me to see it for what it was. It had nothing to do with anyone else, but what I was dealing with on the inside, mentally and emotionally. God had delivered me from drugs, and now He was doing the same for my mental and emotional stability.

I believe God can use the hands of man to work on the heart and the head. During one of these sessions, I got a sobering revelation of the word of God. (2 Timothy 1:12) became my "life verse," as I have heard it called. "He is able to guard what I have entrusted to Him until the day of His return."

So, I latched onto this truth and the part of the verse I still quote to this day when the enemy tries to bring thoughts of distrust and negativity: "I am sure, that He is able to guard that which I have entrusted to Him." You see I had to turn over all the things I viewed as my responsibility to Christ. That included my spouse, my house, my children, and the ministry. *If God is unable to keep you, then you can't be kept!*

I know that sounds simplistic to some, but for me that was freeing. I had been so busy worrying about losing what I thought belonged to me. When I realized none of it belonged to me, my focus then became getting to know the one to whom I was entrusting all my cares. Now, this does not mean the fight was over just because I talked to someone. The battle had just begun.

In the mental and emotional health arena, everyone's battle is the same. It requires that we learn how to maintain patterns of consistency, and a commitment to a sustainable program while rebuilding bridges of trust with those we have harmed, unintentionally in most cases. We cannot expect to put away some fifteen, twenty or more years of emotional pain overnight. It takes time to form new habits, to recognize the things that cause us to gravitate to those things or people that push us toward negative behaviors.

One of the hardest patterns to change is the need for affirmation from people. A pattern for many who have been abused in some way is the need to please others. In my own life I had noticed a constant need for affirmation and reminders from others about worthiness, which can and often does lead to attracting people who can exploit and manipulate that desire for approval. There are many things I allowed from people who were my friends, because I had such a need for their affirmation. I call this the "man-pleaser mode," where all self-regard is abandoned and others are allowed to treat you any kind of way, and they do so knowingly because you will allow them to.

I know you might be thinking I'm only talking about personal relationships, but we have ministry relationships just like that too. Such people are your friends if you are useful to them. No need for real relationships here because they are based solely upon a need. When the need is completed or fulfilled, you are no longer a necessity. This is a good lesson for young pastors to learn early in ministry.

So, we have been given the responsibility of rightly dividing and giving the word of truth to others, but does that mean we are no longer being processed by God concerning our own personal issues? The unwritten rules of ministry are the reason why so many of us do not get the help we need. I have found that people will place spiritual leaders on a pedestal and impose expectations on them that the Bible never required of a spiritual leader. The Hebrew scriptures contained a provision that required spiritual leaders to make offerings for their own sins to cleanse them prior to going to God on behalf of the people.

Why is it that when a member falls into sin there is grace for that, but when a leader falls into sin, he or she must be crucified rather than extended the same grace that Christ died to bestow on all believers? Amen!

We understand the *what*, but let's talk about the *why*. Why do so many people in the body of Christ continue to struggle with the things with which we have always struggled? We know there is a provision for our healing in the word of God, right? We know that when God speaks of healing, He is not only speaking of our physical body, but also our mental and emotional health.

So, we know and understand the word of God. But what is the *why*? I would say, for many it's unrecognized or unadmitted mental and emotional traumas. Every one of us has a story to tell about being disciplined by a parent, and in that moment we might have thought they were trying to kill us. For some, however, this is a real scenario.

Imagine growing up in a Christian household, and while discipline is a concept of God, maybe some of us had a parent suffering with their own mental and emotional issues, so the outpouring of that discipline was not always loving, but unintentionally destructive. We say we have forgiven those past hurts or grievances, but we just learn to better manage them. I'm not just talking about the hurts we experienced at home while we were growing up, but also those wounds we have gotten while walking with the people of God in ministry.

I, like many at an early age, had a jaded view of the church, God, and the spiritual stuff. I didn't know the evil things people in church were capable of, yes, even after they had received Christ. I went into ministry with the same naivete about what "being called" meant. As a pastor, not dealing with unhealthy emotions can lead to the inability to trust people. This can eventually lead to hurting those we have been tasked with helping to heal. So many of us go into ministry, and we just place our hurts and the pain aside and keep it moving. We throw ourselves into the work of the ministry as a form of pain management.

Pain management is simply getting the issues down to an acceptable level of discomfort, nothing more and nothing less. So, the outward signs and symptoms of the issues decrease, and the untimely breakdowns may not occur as often, which equals "pain management." Many of my failures in ministry came at a heavy price, which usually meant hurting people.

We cannot escape the things in us that God is working on. You say, "I have been in ministry for years. My issues have never seemed to cause a problem." I used to feel the same way as you do, but here's what I found out: you cannot separate your spiritual understanding from your mental and emotional self.

God has been working to get our minds right with us since salvation. "The mind is a terrible thing" is a saying I heard once. However, this speaks to the issue: your body is bound to the spirit, so the issues of the mind will affect the spiritual understanding, whether we agree with it or not. Our emotional state plays a big part in how we see our God, and how we see our circumstances. Most people's take on mental health issues are limited unless they themselves or someone they know has been affected by it. For many, their view of mental and emotional health is based solely upon scenarios they have seen depicted in movies and television. The truth is that there are varying degrees of mental and emotional issues.

For example, if we see a young person who is introverted, withdrawn, with unusual and erratic behavior, most of us would look at that young person and agree, "There is something wrong here." That young person could be withdrawn and shy because they witnessed the death of a parent in a car accident and chose to withdraw. It's hard to trust when you are hurting, so that's not a mental issue, that's an emotional one. The other side to that coin is that young person could also be withdrawn from dealing with serious mental issues stemming from severe trauma as a child. They could be a ticking time bomb waiting for someone or something to trigger them. Now that's a mental issue. So, the church must recognize its indifference and develop ministries that address the needs of its community. Why should a believer need to go to the world to find someone to talk to?

There are enough mental and emotional health issues in the church to keep any mental health professional busy for years. For the many people suffering from these issues in the church, all they need is someone to talk to, to help them develop a consistent strategy for care, and steps to maintain deliverance. Yet what about the rare few who are at the other end of the spectrum? They need Jesus too. Yet with our dissociative thinking, we lump all scenarios together because it's easier to ignore what we do not accept as our responsibility.

Let's face it: people in the church are dealing with mental and emotional issues and it's not going away because we were all born into a broken world.

So, what does that look like in the pulpit? For me, it was a continual string of failures. *Wait a minute:* if God told us to do something, and it failed, was that really

God? The answer to that question is yes, we heard God perfectly. So why did it fail, then?

Whatever God calls for will work and continues to work. If it failed, we must learn to find the flesh in the matter meaning: *what desires of mine got in the way of what God wanted?* Many of us at this point chalk the failure up to fact that we missed the mark because we misunderstood God's timing. Then we go back to thinking and doing what we have always done. When we do not ask the right questions, we will continually get the wrong answers.

The real question I should have been asking is not what, but *why* it failed. For me, and I'm sure for many of you reading this book, it is because "my way" got in the way of what God was doing. Now I know you don't have to have mental or emotional issues to have that happen, but for me this was a constant trigger for failures in my ministry career.

Subconsciously, I would find a way to derail the progress we were making. Continued bouts of self-sabotage and self-hatred would routinely cause me to shrink back from God-sized opportunities. My ministry colleagues would often ask me why I hadn't moved into the next level God was showing me. It was because of the internal view I had of myself. I did not want the scrutiny that would follow from making the move because I did not like what I saw in the mirror. I knew that if I moved out into the light, people would be able detect my inner issues with worthiness!

"But," you say, "who *is* worthy?" My question then becomes: If God knows I'm having these challenges, why doesn't He just wait until I get it together?

Beloved, we are all learning to navigate the hard places in our lives, but this does not disqualify us from serving the Lord in a greater capacity. The real question is: Can we be effective in leading others while we are dealing with our own issues? Managing self and managing others are two different skills sets. Just because you have mastered one does not automatically mean you have mastered the other.

Christian Leadership expert Dr. John Maxwell says it like this: "We teach what we know but reproduce who we are." Knowing and admitting we need work in our mental or emotional areas is a crucial step in bringing that much needed balance to our lives. For years I denied there was anything wrong with me because most of the time I was fine. You will never fix or review anything that you consider to be fine in your life.

I went to a twelve step program years ago, and the first principle in a twelve-step program is admitting you are addicted, and you are powerless to do anything about it. The lesson is the same with mental and emotional health issues: you will not address what you do not believe is a problem. So, what do we do?

Well, in those so-called "breakdown moments," it's important to identify contributory factors that may cause you to decline into your breakdowns. Name your triggers. What are they? Are they people, times of the year, or strongly associated with the death of a friend or loved ones? Are you currently under an inordinate amount of stress?

When you ask the right questions, you get the right answers. Here are some additional important questions to ask yourself: How do you feel when you recognize that your breakdown is starting? Can you articulate to someone how you are feeling? Remember, isolation in these times can be very harmful, and you need those around you who can help you to decide what's real from what you feel. Early recognition of triggers can go a long way in creating a sustainable program without the need for medical therapies.

Let's talk about that for a minute. I have heard both schools of thought about believers taking medications for behavioral modification. I have heard that there is no need for it since the provision for our healing and deliverance has already been granted. But I also recognize the principle that I learned in the Bible, how God sends the solution based upon the size of the problem. As a spiritual leader, if a member asked my thoughts on whether they should consider putting their child on a medical therapy for mental disorders because they are routinely a danger to themselves and others, I would have to refer to the wisdom of the God example. What would parents pay to see their children healed, delivered, and set free? God did not spare any expense to see us saved, I could not be mad at believers who did the same for their children. Just a thought!

I do believe there is a balance, don't just give them medication, give them Jesus too; it's their relationship with Him that will bring the stability that they so desperately need. So, to everything there is a balance. In my own experience I have found that having a consistently healthy and well-balanced spiritual and natural diet, along with regular physical exercise and proper body care, are a big part of supporting mental stability and goes a long way in bringing the highs and lows closer together. This is especially true for bi-vocational leaders in ministry. Working in the world while effectively working in ministry is a daunting task. We take for granted our physical limitations when we are bi-vocational. Preparing a sermon, sometimes two to three teachings per week along with a sixty-hour managerial work week, and let's not forget the church department meetings, and calls and hospital visits. Did I mention all the family stuff that goes on as well? The boys must get to football practice on time or face discipline by the coach, who just happens to be you. The girls' ballet, cheer, and gymnastics!

All of this can push anyone out of balance. I have known many people who have had mental and emotional breakdowns; the trigger for most of them was being out of balance and not recognizing that was the cause. Even too much church can throw you out of balance. I know right now someone reading this passage is twitching because you didn't know there was a such thing as too much church. *There is never too much God, but there can be too much church*! For some, the church has become a mistress, demanding attention and energy that belongs to your family. Believe me, I know what it's like to have a burning desire to see God's plan for ministry come to pass, but I have learned about this principle called capacity. Your capacity determines your ability to lead, who, and how many you can lead. Many aspire to lead thousands, but if your anointing is only for five hundred, guess what? That's okay, too. I have learned that if you are leading one or 1 million, all God's people are what's most valuable to Him. Let us not fall into the trap of bigger and better for the sake of bigger and better and calling it God.

Now, there is nothing more frustrating that putting all your efforts into seeing a ministry grow, and yet nothing appears to be happening while other ministries around you are just exploding with growth. The greatest lesson I have learned in ministry is that you are not called to everyone. This can throw you and your ministry off balance. What do I mean? For years, it seemed like we got the people nobody else wanted. My wife and I would often joke about being anointed for broken people, because they were all we seemed to attract. Where were all the whole, delivered, and set free people in the body?

We did not know it, but we had been attracting the people God had for us to lead all along. However, we were looking for the "not so crazy people." We all have missed some ministry opportunities here because people with mental and emotional issues need Jesus too. Being out of balance affects your mental and emotional wellbeing.

There are church leaders right now who have a phone glued to their hands. I mean right now while you are reading this book, you just stopped to check your text messages, or tweets, or IG's because social media has programmed us to prioritize it over everything else. I want us to wake up to the realities of our own mental and emotional limitations.

If the organizations we are leading cannot run without us, then we have failed as leaders. The duplication of your efforts should be a priority for every leader in whatever capacity you serve. If you are a greeter or a preacher, your goals is to reproduce. I understand. No one cares about the baby like you do. But this type of mentality breeds behaviors that lead us to being out of balance. Let me say this: we don't have to put people in position just because we need a warm body there. Take some of the ministry departments off your website. It is okay to not have that ministry if you don't have competent people to lead it. This can cause you more frustration and stress than you could ever imagine. Sometimes we as pastors have put people into positions they were not anointed for or possessed the required skills. Can they learn? Well, that depends on their capacity for learning.

I am finding as we move further into the digital media age that some candidates will not be able to participate in some facets of ministry for you if they are unwilling to embrace and learn recent technology. As leaders, we must make the tough decisions. I know Sister Mary wants to sing in the choir, but she can't sing! Stop putting people in positions they are not qualified or anointed for. This will make it so much easier on you later because you won't have to deal with the "I'm leaving the church mad" conversations, because she got wounded because we did not tell her the truth. I would rather such people get angry and leave in truth, than leave and allow a lie to carry forward. In this particular person's case, wherever she goes, she still won't be anointed to sing.

# Chapter 2

# The Birth of The Brokenness

## *The Absence Of Information Births Improvisation*

You have seen them, especially if you have been around church like I have. Everyone in the church knows there is something different about Sister Mary Lou. Nobody really talks about it; that would not be very Christ-like, now would it? And let's not even talk about what we say about them at the dinner table on Sundays.

"Did you see Sister Mary Lou throw her Bible up onto the pulpit today? Man, she is '**crazy**"! And they laugh and talk about all the things that had happened in service that morning.

As the leader, your after service experience is a little different. You have just preached the most powerful sermon of your pastoral career. People were saved, delivered, and set free, but you find yourself in a state of uncontrollable weeping; not because you are happy about people giving their lives to Christ, they haven't noticed it because you hide it so well, but you are one of those "**crazy**" people too. People got their healing, but you are still waiting on yours. It's Monday morning now, the anointing lifts off you, and you are left with your own thoughts. The mind begins to question whether you really did "preach" like everybody said. Did I miss it? Was there too much flesh in the message? Never mind the fact people got saved! The mind begins to question the reason you keep on doing "this"! Are you good enough? Do you have enough to fulfill the assignment God has given you? Why is this thing not growing? The problem is not that you don't have the qualifications, or that you haven't been tested in your faith. Nor does there appear to be anything wrong in the ministry. I know what you are thinking: Doesn't this happen to all of us in ministry?

Correct, but imagine someone struggling with mental or emotional issues having the same internal dialogue. I want us to recognize that this may be a continual battle for many. Those old thoughts just seem to linger in the back of one's mind. These are like words carved into the top of an old, dusty desktop stored up in the attic. The carvings are a reminder of the traumatic experiences you have endured. The carvings say molestation, physical abuse, verbal, and emotional abuse. Too often, those who are struggling with their mental and emotional health issues are fighting a losing battle, and they are alone. It's like situations in the Hebrew scriptures. Many believed that if something bad happened to you, then you or someone in your family did something wrong, or that you were cursed. Many of the people of God I have met who deal with mental and emotional issues are byproducts of serious parental or familial traumas. Childhood wounds that we in the church had failed to recognize. Many have carried this baggage for years. It's time for them to take the baggage out of the car and leave at the altar!

**But let's start at the beginning …**
**The birth of the brokenness!**

Where did the brokenness start? Ever since I can remember, church just seemed to connect with me. I loved singing and going to church. The Bible just made sense to me. I would get new revelations, visions, and dreams, and worship songs would routinely ring in my heart. These are my earliest memories of what being "called" by God looked like. Everyone told me God was going to use me in a mighty way. I was allowed to sing in the adult choir, they let me lead the youth day programs, but it seemed that no one ever bothered to find out if I was okay. No one seemed to recognize the secret cries for help, needing someone to save me from the pain I was experiencing at home. This happens many times in many church circles. Young ministry gifts are put before the ministry community, sometimes just too early. But no one ever really cares enough to ask about the mental, and emotional state of those young ministers. For those who could see, maybe when dealing with other believers' children, that subject was secretly off the table?

These children have become some of the most anointed and powerful men and women of God in the church today, but they often suffer with bouts of depression, suicidal thoughts, sexual identity issues, infidelity, and other self-destructive patterns brought on by childhood traumas. They are powerful ministry gifts seeing people get saved and delivered, but they themselves need to be delivered and set free! They are ***Blessed and Broken*** on the inside.

I grew up in the inner city of Atlanta, Georgia, in an area not too far from Morris Brown College. I attended the M. Agnes Jones Elementary school as a young boy, along with my younger sister. The public housing projects we grew up in taught me some valuable lessons. The most impactful one was that I was different from those around me. I never quite fit in with those I went to school with. I was the same color. I had the same back story as many: young black boy raised by a single mother in the inner city. But because of the influences around me, I started smoking cigarettes, drinking, and taking part in petty thefts with the older boys. Mind you, I was only six or seven years old at the time. I became the narrative.

When I was nine years old, my mother met and married a working-class divorcee with five children of his own. He owned a home in the Baywood suburbs of Atlanta. My mother told me years later that she married him because he was a good provider. My stepfather worked as an electrician and freelanced on the side doing A/C and electrical work. My mother worked for a local book manufacturer at the time. By the standards of the current world, we were a lower middle-class family. Our neighborhood was mostly made up of two-parent, two-income households.

No matter where I was, I found myself fitting in with "the crowd." The fitting in does not make this story interesting, but the lengths I would go through to "fit in." I had become a type of chameleon. Fitting in wherever was what I was able to do. I had learned to become whoever I saw, even down to mimicking voices I heard on television. I could walk like them, talk like them, act like them, and yes, even sing like them. I was a perfect copy of the originals. My only reason for doing this was to gain people's attention. I liked that "feeling" that came from someone telling me I was "funny," or that I was "so cute," or that I was a "really smart" young man. Simply put, I was looking for someone to affirm that I mattered. I was looking for the affirmation that can only come from a father.

*The absence of information births improvisation.* These types of behaviors often come from not knowing your identity or your purpose. If you take a seed, and plant it in a dark place with only one source of light, that plant will grow toward that source of light. So as a young man, I was not told how important my uniqueness was.

This uniqueness made me who I was. Every young person needs that affirmation of a father, whether male or female. No one told me that being different was a true commodity, and this caused me to seek to fit in. Why? Because no one else around me was like me. They did not see what I saw, they didn't think like I thought. My thought process was always beyond where I was. I told my mother once I saw myself wealthy, and living in a big house one day, and that I would travel the world singing. She told me to "be quiet, you are too high-minded!"

Negative affirmation only fueled my desire to fit in even more. No one celebrates the "unique" child. A child grows to the strongest source of encouragement, just as that seed planted in the dark grows toward its only source of light. I often remember hearing my mother tell others that I was always a loving child. Interpreted, she was saying I always needed to hear someone tell me they loved me. I gave love to receive it back because I wanted to matter. Affirmation was the language I needed to become what I saw in my mind. I needed someone to tell me it was okay to be the way I was. I needed to hear that I wasn't weird, or crazy, and that the things I saw in my dreams were real and I could be anything I wanted to be.

As I mentioned earlier in the chapter, my stepfather was an excellent provider, but being an excellent provider does not guarantee someone is an excellent parent. His child-rearing philosophy was of the old adage, "A child should be seen, and not heard." He ruled with an iron fist, and a staunch belief that a slap to the face, or a tree branch or extension cord to the rear, would cure all our childhood behavioral issues.

He was a short man with an inferiority complex, married to a beautiful six-foot-tall Amazon woman, and yes, she was dealing with her own depression and self-esteem issues too. He had obsessive-compulsive issues that routinely meant swift punishment for not cleaning up properly or not putting things back in an orderly fashion. Oddly, this would help me years later in my operational management career because I had such an eye for detail.

His name for me as a child was "Dummy." He called me that so much, my friends around the neighborhood thought he was calling me "Donnie," like a nick name. This affected me in so many ways in my young adult life. Years later, a supervisor on the job complemented me on figuring out how to improve an antiquated work process. She told me that I was intelligent, at which I wondered, "Who is she talking about? Me?" I thought I was dumb and was not worthy of that kind of praise.

I had been programmed to hate myself, even though I was highly intelligent.

Now, I understand children should be disciplined for wrongful actions, and this is necessary for that child to grow, but I have also learned that a dose of balance and grace and love are necessary in the process.

I often felt abandoned by my mother. How could she allow this man to abuse her children like that? This was coupled with constant abuse from our stepsiblings, because my sister and I were the outsiders, and they perceived us as a threat coming in to take their father away from them. I would often tell my sister I was leaving and going back to the Projects where I belonged. I did not feel anyone wanted me there, and I would often try to convince her to come along with me. I was fed up with the physical and verbal abuse and told my stepfather I was leaving and going back to the Projects, to which he replied, "I'll help you pack!"

I got as far as the end the street and realized I did not have anywhere to go. I returned to the house, and sat on the front porch until it was dark, not wanting to go back in. My mother came to the door and asked me if I was hungry. I told her no, but my stomach was really growling by that time. She called my name, as only a mother could, and told me getting something to eat would make me feel better. When I went back inside, my stepfather smugly asked me "I thought you were going back to the Projects?" My mom told him to leave me alone. I came back in, at least at that moment feeling that she really loved me.

Later, my stepfather's eighteen-year-old nephew came to live with us for a while. It seems that he was having some issues at home and was sent to my stepfather to be "straightened out." He was, to say the least, a bad influence on me. He became my roommate and would often encourage me to steal things for him, and of course, mister "want to fit in" happily obliged because he showed me attention.

Then he began abusing me sexually and physically. Finally, it came to the point that I refused to do what he was telling me to do. He threatened to tell everyone what I had been doing, and when they found out, everyone would hate me, and no one would ever love me if they found out. Imagine the fear and dread I felt at that moment.

The encounters became even more violent when I began to fight back. I no longer did what he told me to do, bringing the situation to the point of him hitting and choking me. By chance, my mother walked in our room one night and caught him smothering me under a pillow, and effectively administered a beatdown of epic proportion! I can only assume that he went back home. I'm not sure. I just saw my stepfather help him pack his bags, and he took him somewhere. I can remember him staring at me as if to say, "This is your fault." And while

I was certainly relieved that he was gone, there was this overwhelming sense of dread that I was all alone again.

Now mind you, my sister, and stepsiblings were there, but I felt like my sister, and I were on the same boat in the middle of the ocean. The encounters with my stepfather's nephew changed me more than I realized. I found myself alienated from those around me. At school I had become the object of hatred, for some reason. Why was there so much hatred toward me? I didn't understand it then as I do today: it was because I had begun to display very effeminate qualities, which of course in that day meant nobody liked you. I would often get into fights. Well, I wouldn't necessarily call them fights. They were more like beat downs because nobody wanted to be around someone who was "sweet," as they used to call it. So, in my early teen years I was really battling a crisis of identity.

While I have spared my readers many of the more intricate details of my childhood emotional traumas, this narrative should serve as a wakeup call to the church to recognize and address concerns over children who display signs of child abuse or molestation in our congregations. We must train the workers who interact with our children to observe and report anything they might consider suspicious. This includes deep discolored bruises, cuts, burns, or unusual dissociative patterns. These children are crying out for someone to recognize that they are hurting. We have the responsibility to let them know they are not alone, and that someone notices and cares.

I know we are on a slippery slope on this subject, but I would rather be wrong and have the accused person upset with me, than not do or say anything, and have a child suffer and even be murdered. This is a very unfortunate but real scenario in our world today.

Even though I was experiencing a lot of negativities in my young life, I never forgot the words that were spoken over me about my calling. My stepfather was installing a drop ceiling and light fixtures in the pastor's office at the church one Saturday afternoon, and I had the opportunity to follow the pastor around while he completed some of his tasks in the church. Our conversation was light and whimsical. He asked me what I wanted to be when I grew up.

I told him, "I want to do what you do."

He said, "For real, you want to be a preacher?"

In answer, I nodded my head confidently. After we returned to his office, he asked me again in front of my stepfather what I wanted to be when I grew up. I held my head in shame and said I wanted to be an electrician. Of course, I didn't really want to be an electrician like him. I'm not sure if the pastor recognized the signs I was displaying. I was afraid of my stepfather because of the abuse we were suffering at home. I had learned early on how to play the ego game, telling people what they wanted to hear to avoid conflict. I had a constant fear that he would find something wrong, resulting in me getting a slap to the face or to the mouth. And let's not even talk about the creative kinds of punishments that awaited us when we were in trouble.

When you are young and called to ministry, you are usually different from most of the other children around you. There are signs, yes, even in the troubled ones like me. There is usually a wakeup call of sorts where the Holy Spirit will give you a glimpse of your destiny. I didn't understand how special and unique I was, but God had greater plans for me. I received Christ at the age of 12 years old and I can remember routinely experiencing dreams of being held down and smothered. I learned from my grandmother this happens sometimes to young believers when called to ministry, she called it "the witch riding you." Basically, it's a demonic tactic whereby the enemy attempts to instill fear through intimidation. It was undeniable God was doing something special with me.

One Sunday morning, my Sunday school teacher asked me to stand out in the hall because I was being disruptive in class. One of the deacons came and talked to me and asked me why I was being so disruptive. I boldly told him the stuff they were teaching was baby stuff, and it was too easy for me! The deacon took me into the adult Sunday school class and gave me a book to follow along. He was trying to intimidate me, but I loved it! I would take my book and read it at home, study and do my homework, and I would have questions to ask in class. Mind you, I was the only young person in the adult Bible study class.

I began to practice with the adult choir, and eventually was asked to join the communion team, which we served every Sunday. Eventually, I was promoted to Sunday evening communion leader, and after that able to lead on Sunday mornings. I started working at the church on a part-time basis, assisting with the cleaning duties. When the custodian moved away due to work reassignment, I was given his job with pay. Church was that exciting escape I needed, and as far as I could tell, most people did not know what was going on at home.

As I started to get older, I got to that place where I was tired of that man hitting on me. I decided since he was not going to leave on his own, I was going to help him on his way. One Sunday afternoon, as my mother prepared dinner, I took some of my stepdad's nitro glycerin pills, which he took for a heart condition, and put them into the sweet potatoes my mother was simmering for dinner. I had found out in science class that dynamite was made using nitro glycerin, so I figured if I poured enough of them into the sweet potatoes, his heart would explode.

Don't you dare judge me! I told my little sister not to eat the sweet potatoes that night. About fifteen minutes later, my mother called me into the kitchen and showed me the undissolved pills in the bottom of the sweet potato pan and poured them down the sink. She was not angry, but her face showed disappointment. I was afraid she was going to tell him what I had done, but she didn't.

When she served him his dinner he asked, "Where are the sweet potatoes?"

My mother replied, "I burned them and had to throw them away."

He said, "How did you do that?"

"I was on the phone and forgot about them."

He had some "colorful metaphors" about her being on the phone so much. She took one for me. In retrospect, I now realize she had figured out that I was tired of his abuse to me, my sister, and my mother as well.

Not only was he physically abusive, but verbally and mentally as well. I was tired of him hurting us! The situation finally came to a head one evening. He hit me again, and I tried to grab something and hit him with it, and I yelled, "I'm tired of you hitting on me!"

My mother grabbed me and whispered in my ear, "It's time to go, baby." She had finally realized it was time for us to leave.

My stepdad would routinely work out of town, and when he was gone one week, my mother moved us into an apartment on the other side of town. He did eventually find out where we lived and came and took my mother's car, and my little half-brother they had together.

I saw my mother struggle to make ends meet. But from that I learned how to persevere. I saw this man do everything he could to destroy my mother, but we were finally free!

If you are a parent reading this book, remember that your words are the pavement your children travel on. You decide how rocky that road is going to be for them. I have learned through experience when disciplining my own children, words are immensely powerful tools that can shape the mindset of a child. Be mindful that correction in anger has the possibility to be destructive rather than constructive, and we must always temper correction with grace and love.

It's a good practice after disciplining your children to go back and talk about it, and explain, and reassure them why the correction is necessary. Most of all, a hug of encouragement goes a long way to solidify the lessons taught through correction.

If you are part of my generation, you have heard the old saying, "There is no parenting manual," which I have found to be true. No two children are alike, and our parental responsibility is to discover what motivates, stimulates, and sometimes deters children from getting in their own way. Remember, if you see things in your children that you do not like, they are a byproduct of what they have seen in you. Children will do 5 percent of what you say, and 95 percent of what you see you do. I grew up in a home that going to church was a normal thing, but it did not mean my parental figures were always living what they preached.

Can your children say the same about you?

# Chapter 3

# Chance Encounters

It was the first day of middle school registration. I was so excited about the possibility of making new friends, and more importantly, no one knew my past so I could be whoever I wanted to be. At this new school I would have the "Chance Encounter" that changed my life.

Mom had finally gotten the courage to leave behind my stepfather and his abusive ways. We moved to an area in the suburbs of Atlanta known as East Point. We were registering me for school, but we did not know this would lead to a chance encounter with my biological father.

"Pop" was tall, about six-foot-four-inches, with a strong build and mocha brown skin. He was wearing a black shirt with slacks, a beaded Indian headband around his head, and cowboy boots. When I saw him from a distance, I thought it was odd for a black man to be dressed like an Indian. He was standing near the entrance of the school as we approached, and he greeted my mother with a pleasant hug. He asked me if I remembered who he was.

My mother said, "He is not going to remember you."

To her surprise, and for reasons I am not sure of, I knew exactly who he was, and said, "You are my father."

In response, my father exclaimed happily, "I knew that he would remember me after all these years!"

My mother asked him what he was doing there, and he told her that he had re-married, and his new wife had two children of her own, a girl and a boy. He was there registering her son for school. *Wow, you mean I have a stepbrother.* Great, I would not be alone at this new school. In fact, he told us my brother was walking toward us right then. I looked and I saw several students, but I could not pick out the one that was my brother.

My father said, "Right there, he's the white kid."

Oh my God! You mean to tell me my dad was married to a "white woman"! My mind was going in circles at that point, trying to get a handle on the moment. My stepbrother was lanky with long, greasy hair, and looked a lot like a surfer to me. When my dad told him who I was, he reached out and hugged me happily. He said "Pop" had always told them about us and that one day we would meet. He was extremely excited to meet us.

I want you to understand that at this point, I had little trust for white people, and didn't really know how I felt about the situation. My encounters with white people were limited to what I saw on television. I never saw white people in the areas where I grew up. My father asked, since we had a few weeks before school started, could my sister and I come stay with them to get better acquainted with our new stepsiblings, as I referred to them. When I did so, my father would often say, "I don't have any stepchildren in my family, because we don't step on anybody!"

At this point, I really didn't know how I felt. The car ride home was noticeably quiet. My mother asked me what I thought about my dad.

"I don't know, he seems kind of weird… Why is he wearing an Indian headband and cowboy boots?" I wasn't sure I wanted to be around those "white" people. I told her I would be willing for just for one day on the weekend.

In retrospect, I can see what my mother liked about my father; classic bad boy/good girl scenario, we always want what we shouldn't have. They had met working on the job together at Grady Memorial Hospital in Atlanta, he was a paramedic, and my mom was a secretary. So, my mother arranged for my sister and me to meet our father and our two stepsiblings on a Saturday. We met them at an arcade on Sylvan Road in East Point. When I saw them in action, quite frankly I thought they were not very well-mannered or well-behaved. They were running around the arcade like they owned the place. I played a few games but didn't want to ask my father for too much money like the others were doing. They were going through quarters like they were going out of style.

I sat at the concession bar and watched as the others played. My father asked me if I was hungry. He said I could have anything I wanted. I really didn't want to ask him for anything because I didn't want to seem greedy.

He handed me a stack of quarters and said, "Why don't you go and play with your brother and sisters?"

I told him I didn't want to be wasteful and spend all that money on video games. He whispered something that totally set me free.

He said, "It's okay if you spend money in here. I know the owner… it's me," with a smile, and a laugh.

Are you kidding me? My dad owns an arcade… awesome!

Notice how I had taken on ownership. He had moved from being my father to being my dad in that very instant.

Once school started, the weekend visits were less frequent. I immersed myself in the new culture of the school. How many of you know I started hanging with the "on the way to trouble or dead" crowd? I began smoking weed, cutting classes, and skipping school on occasion. Some of the members from a local street gang "Down By Law" had started to hang around, and I was acting like they were acting. It was only a matter of time before I got "jumped in." The final straw was me coming home high and drunk.

My mother was fed up with my delinquent ways and decided to send me to live with my father for good. This happened at the right time because I was on my way to trouble for sure. While sending me to my father in that moment may have seemed like a punishment to me, it was just what I needed. My father had a different kind of discipline style than the one I had become accustomed to. I remember once getting into trouble and I asked my dad, *Are you going to beat me too?*

You see, children who have been abused tend to expect the worst. Really, the acting out was a sign of rebellion because I didn't feel loved. My misdeeds were about gaining the attention of my parents, even if that meant the attention was negative.

My father showed me something I had never experienced before. He recognized that the traumas I had suffered at the hands of my stepfather and others had birthed something in me that he did not like.

I remember him saying to me one day, "No son of mine is going to walking around with a <u>bent wrist</u>!" He showed me how a man walks, and how a man sits. He taught me how to dress, how to tie a tie, and we all had to learn to box to defend ourselves. If you were the children of a blended family, going to school in a predominantly black neighborhood in those days, you'd better know how to fight. He gave me what I had so been longing for: that male impartation and affirmation. I'm not saying my father was the perfect male role model, but up to this point he was the best one I had encountered.

My greatest challenge with me going to live with Dad for good was that I had to learn to trust white people. My stepmother and brothers never treated us bad, but the negative stigma I had about them was based upon limited information. I found out that white people love collard greens, black-eyed peas, and smothered porkchops like the next person, I just had to add a little more salt to-everything....

My dad had his own messed-up way and thought processes about how life should work. He chose a different method of punishment. He punished me with love, which meant doing pushups, cleaning up the house, and being on "restrictions," as he called them. But he always came back and explained why he did what he did and gave hugs and kisses to all of us when he had to punish us. In fact, I can remember my father only hitting me once in the six years I lived with him.

One Friday night, I stayed out too late after a football game and tried to sneak in the window. My father was up and there to meet me. The next morning, I tried sleeping in late. My father came into the room and smacked me on the behind and said, "Get up out that bed! You are not going to sleep the day away!"

To us, my father was "Pop," that loving type of man I was not used to. But don't be fooled. There was another side of him. Everyone on the outside of the family who knew my father knew he was not somebody you wanted to mess with! My father's older sons from a previous marriage to their mother had aptly named him "Crazy Horse," that mean street guy. Crazy Horse was the cussing, vodka-drinking, cigarette-smoking, gun-toting, crazy-Indian man nobody messed with.

My father routinely carried a gun with him, which didn't set off any alarms to me, as he owned an arcade. But he was a very "enterprising entrepreneur," to say the least. He had "other business ventures" that just happened to keep him busy, usually at night.

We never grow beyond what we have been exposed too, so although I did not agree with my dad's lifestyle, by being around him I learned how to be his interpretation of what a man was. I learned how to speak up for myself, and not allow people to bully me and talk to me any kind of way. I adopted the tough guy persona, at least outwardly. Inwardly, I was still a broken young man. I was just mimicking what I saw. I became the even more screwed-up version of my dad.

I started smoking because he smoked. He would tell me, "Buy your own, don't smoke mine," so if I bought my own cigarettes, he didn't care. I looked much older than I was, and back then you could send your children to the store to buy cigarettes for you. Smoking was not as frowned upon as it is today. But I adopted his hustler mentality, always looking for a quick buck, always working an angle or a scam. From staging car accidents, to slip-and-falls in building halls, we did it all.

As we got older, everybody in the house who was capable of working had to bring some money home. At this point, I felt like my father became my pimp. You could work a regular job or work the street corners, it didn't matter to him, but you'd better bring his money home. He would take my stepbrother and me around the neighborhoods and bill us out for yardwork or cleanup projects, but everybody got their hustle on. If we had a dog, I'm sure it would have had to bring some money home too.

I had gotten a job working at Longhorn Steakhouse with my uncle, who was a chef. I came home late from work one night, and my father asked me where my check was. I had forgotten it was pay day and didn't even go to the office to get my check, because he would usually take it all. I guess I didn't remember because it wasn't really my money. I felt like I was working for free. If you asked him why you could not have any of the money you worked for, he would say, "Everything costs around here," and "If you don't like it, you can start your own 'family.'" That was what he called us, "The Family," modeled after some of the Italian crime families depicted on television, I'm sure. So, I left my father's house angry and misguided. The potential for greatness was always within me, but now it was even more misguided.

# Chapter 4

# You Got To Be A Man Now

I left my father's house at the ripe old age of nineteen, after having dropped out of college for a vocal performance degree. I did not go back after my first year because my stepmother fell ill, and my father told me it was my responsibility to take up the slack. Of course, you know that this did not set well with my mother. It caused a rift in our relationship because I had to tell her, *it's my life and my decision.* I was really starting to want my independence. I had gotten to the place where I did not like either of their rules, so I started my own "family." That was one of his greatest sayings: "If you don't like the way I run my household, please feel free to start your own!" (I quote this to my own sons!)

So, with my hustle skills, and the entrepreneurial acumen I had learned from "Pop," and the work ethic instilled in me by my abusive stepfather, I undertook my new life. I had a car, a couch I bought from my brother, my girlfriend, and the clothes on our backs, and we headed out.

Enter the "Hustle Man" because *you got to be a man now*! I was young and had gained a strong attitude of self-reliance, although misguided, and a huge chip on my shoulder. I was going to prove everyone wrong who had ever doubted me, abused me, hurt me, and talked down to me! I was the smartest dumb guy you would have ever met.

By this time, I was really done with the church. The final straw for me came when my youth pastor came before the congregation, as was customary in the Church of Christ faith, and confessed fathering a child outside of his marriage.

He and his wife announced they were getting a divorce. At that point, as far as I was concerned, every male figure that had influenced me either abused, misguided, or failed me. I would go to church every now and then when mom would ask me to, but I didn't feel comfortable there anymore. I didn't feel like hearing the "we're so disappointed in you" conversations I would have with some of the deacons who had trained me when I was younger.

"How did you fall so far away from the faith?"

One of them even asked me at the hospital on my mother's death bed, "What happened to you? We just knew that you were going to be a "mighty preacher" one day."

Now mind you, I was already walking in ministry as a young pastor at the time, but because I wasn't part of the Church of Christ faith, I was not considered to be a "mighty preacher."

"You would dare to speak to me like that, and my mom is lying here, about to die? You know what? Get out of my face, because all of you talk a good game, but none of you are the real deal.

Actually, I said that in my head. Verbally, I responded simply, "Jesus is Lord to the glory of God the Father," and left it at that.

I was tired of seeing the imitation men of God, from my stepfather, who was a deacon, to my youth pastor, to the other deacons at my old church. I had shut down that inner voice as much as I could because I didn't want to hear the Holy Spirit talking to me anymore.

I put Hustle Man to work. I talked myself into a decent job because I dressed and "sounded" like I knew what I was talking about, but I didn't have a clue what I was doing. I learned the jobs as I did them. If I could get in front of you, I knew I would get the job.

My first real job was working for a major credit card firm as a credit analyst. I purposely added this encounter because I want you to see how my unresolved childhood issues affected me into my young adult life. Especially when things started going well.

We answered phones and took credit application information for customers applying for credit. Now, it may sound like a very boring job, but at that time the amount of money I was making was above the national average. I was able to get my girlfriend on with the company as well. Together, we brought home a nice salary. Things were looking up. We started to party with our work friends. We were all young, had money, no kids, and were on our own, so we banded together. We would often travel from house to house every weekend, partying.

This was a nonstop process. We all had money, no responsibilities, and we were living our "best life," as I heard it said recently. Our weeks routinely consisted of work Monday through Thursday, and partying Friday through Sunday, and sometimes Thursday through Sunday, and sometimes Sunday would turn into Monday after work, and Tuesday, and Wednesday after work. We spent a lot of time with our newfound friends. I started selling drugs to make a little extra money on the side. This led me into selling harder drugs, which led me into my own addiction.

There is a rule in the drug game: "You don't get high on your own supply!" But you know me, I had to defy the odds, and found myself secretly out of control with my addiction. This was the major reason my relationship with my eldest son's mother did not work out. I was too busy hanging in the streets and not spending enough time at home with my newborn son and soon to be ex-fiancé.

Now, I still went to work every day though. I was the functioning addict. I was excelling on the job too.

People were recognizing my potential and wanted to help me grow in the company. James, the only African American manager at the company, took me under his wing. My desk was across the aisle from his office door, and I would notice him watching and listening to me on the phone sometimes.

I kept thinking; *Something is wrong with this guy. Why does he keep staring at me all the time?* One day he called me into his office and asked me what I wanted to do with my life. I told him that one day I wanted to go into management like him. Hustle Man!

He began to give me advice on how to move up in the company and gave me special projects on the side to help me mature in my current role. I was on my way to the board room, or so I thought. With my newfound freedom and systems access to information, I politely gave myself a revolving credit line and bought me some new furniture. I didn't tell anyone at first. Not even my girlfriend knew how I got the furniture.

I did finally tell one of my so-called friends. Let's just call him "Judas." He was the guy everybody liked in the group. He was usually the life of the party, you know the militant type and always talked about how he was going to stick it to the man, and how the "black man must rise unified as one people"! Judas was my equal at the company. He was receiving some of the same favor and recognition from another manager in the company. He was an intelligent well-dressed young black man with lots of potential for upward mobility as well. But what I did not know was that his manager, Gino, had asked him to catch me on tape disclosing how I was able to assign myself the credit.

Judas asked me for a ride home one day, and he had a tape recorder in his hand. I asked him why he had it, and he said they gave him the recorder to work on his diction. He was from South Georgia, so it did not raise any flags for me, because he had a deep Southern accent. He asked me about how I got the furniture and wanted to pay me to do it for him. I told him I would not sell it to him, but I would set it up for him for free because he was my friend. He kept asking me how I did it, and if anyone on the inside helped me. He was helping the company build a case against me for fraud and theft, and they were looking for my accomplices. Mind you, when the company approached me a couple of weeks later, I was wondering how they knew what I had done. I would have never thought in a million years that my brother "Judas" would sell me out to the "man"!

They fired me on the spot from that job and put me into collections like any other delinquent credit risk. The company could have sent me to jail, but it appears that "someone" suggested otherwise. I have no doubt in my mind that James, my former mentor, had something to do with it.

I know you are wondering how I did it. How did I crack the system? The truth is, I don't even know. I just figured it out, no prior computer training, no prior business experience. I talked my way into that job. I was smart like most criminals. I had the potential to do so many great things, but often settled for the easy way, or tried to con my way through everything because it was the pattern I had learned from my dad.

I was taught that every situation is an opportunity for a hustle. I had watched my dad hustle people so much. It finally dawned on me that although he had some success in business, he never really made it to that next level of success he always talked about. In the hustler game, you must be ruthless and willing to mess over anybody for the purpose of your gain. The problem I had with that was that I had learned to hustle, but I knew in my heart it was wrong. I can remember telling my dad one day: *I want my name to mean something*.

He said to me, "Your name does mean something." I was saying to him that the path he was on looked good right now, but eventually it was not going to lead to the greatness he always talked about.

I did not go to jail for my misdeeds, but I really should have. It was hard finding a full-time job after that. I had spent three years at the credit firm, and it was hard to explain a three-year gap at my age. I was able to get on with some temporary agencies, but it was a while before I was able to entertain any type of full-time offers.

The lesson here is that anything you have not dealt with in your character will show up when greater opportunities reveal themselves. No one "just happens" to mess up great opportunities. Failure is a direct consequence of our own inner health and wealth, meaning when you are fulfilled on the inside, there is no need to manufacture opportunities. You attract into your life what you are. The more committed you are to preparing for the next important thing, the more likely it is you will recognize that for which you have been preparing.

I have found that if your focus has been negativity, then that's what will manifest into your life. No matter how much success you create from doing things the wrong way, it will never bear good fruit. Maybe not today, or tomorrow, but whatever is built on a faulty foundation will crumble. Even when it appears you are winning, somehow, that negativity will find you, and usually shows up at the most inopportune times.

Every decision I made as a young adult was based upon serious mental and emotional issues.

# Chapter 5

# A Legend in My Own Mind

The one thing I was sure of was that I wasn't built to keep working those J.O.B.'s which means "just over broke"! The hustler in me would not allow it. I began following the music scene in Atlanta, which at that time was being referred to as the next music mecca. Companies like LaFace Records and up and coming producers like Dallas Austin and Organized Noize were causing quite a stir in the local Hip Hop music scene. There it was, my opportunity to do what I loved to do: **Sing**!

I started gigging around the local area and did some talent shows, hoping I would get noticed. Of course, you know it didn't work out like I expected. This endeavor really showed me that although I had chosen this path, the call on my life would not allow me to commit fully to the successes the music industry had to offer.

I had gotten in on an open call audition for Rap-A-Lot Records. They are best known for their work with rap groups like The Ghetto Boys, Scarface, and some other nationally known artists. I had the persona, I had the hair, I had the look, and I had the voice to make it in the industry as a singer. My time had come to go before the judges, and I let it rip! The producer was excited and liked my stage name: "Mike Moses - The Big Man."

He said, "Man I like your name! Can you rap?"

I told him I could and spit a piece for him, and he said that was fantastic! "But can you curse?"

Once again, my "calling" was causing conflict between what I wanted to do and what I knew I was supposed to be doing. I told him I wouldn't and left the audition empty-handed. I questioned myself for weeks on end. Should I have taken the gig? Did I miss my "big break"?

A few months later, I was watching VH1, and a new rap artist came out. His name was "Big Mike." The label that introduced the artist was Rap-A-Lot Records, the company for which I had auditioned. It appeared they took part of my name and created a character that went on to have major success in the industry. I felt like I had missed the opportunity of a lifetime. According to those I talked to, I should have "cursed on the raps, made the money, and repented later"!

But that's how bad character works, right? What was interesting, though, was that I would lie, cheat, and steal, but cursing on a song was absolutely out of the question. Go figure that one out. I knew that at some point, my mother or grandmother would hear about it, as if cursing on a rap song was more wrong than lying, stealing, and cheating my way through life. Either way, I would hear about it from them so, I finally concluded that the record company game wasn't geared for the artist to win. I started my own production and management company and managed myself as an artist.

I had become risky and adventurous. I had a zeal, but it was not even in the vicinity of knowledge. I was going to be a "star" in the music industry. I would always say I wanted a gold album, and that became my driving force. I wanted to be a nationally known recording artist. This pursuit led me into some of the dark circles of the music industry. Drug usage among music artists is no new phenomenon. For me, this served as a distraction that kept me from recognizing the real issue with which I was struggling. No addiction starts off as physical. It is always the feeling that gets you before it becomes a physical addiction.

My life was spiraling out of control. I had pulled away from most of the people who cared about me. For several years I stayed in this cycle of just enough, where I would just go to work and buy drugs and make it to my talent shows. That was enough. But that type of lifestyle will only lead to places you never intended to go.

I was seeing some local success, and I had a halfway decent temporary work assignment, but eventually it was going to crash in on me. I was an accident going somewhere to happen. My life had become very radical, and my emotions were all over place. Often, I would have fits of road rage. If someone honked their horn at me, I would boldly get out of the car and ask the other driver if they had a problem with their horn. I walked around not really caring about anything or anybody, not even myself. It was like I wanted to die.

Eventually, I got tired of the limited success I had experienced on the R & B scene and let that fall to the wayside, as per my usual. This was the recurring theme in my life. I could never seem to complete anything I started. I would start ventures with great enthusiasm but would allow them to fall to the wayside when things got hard, or they were just not interesting to me anymore. I always questioned whether I could have really made it in the music industry had I actually stuck with it.

I realize now that if I had gotten the success I wanted, I would not be alive to author this book.

Sure, everyone goes through a little discouragement sometimes. That's a part of life. But for me, the continual inability to stay on task or to complete what I had started was a constant theme in my life. I didn't know it at the time, but this was part of a greater issue in dealing with my emotional issues.

Mental health is such a taboo subject in the body of Christ. So many of us limp on, hoping that one day we will be free. Early on, I dealt with my issues by throwing myself further into my addiction to anesthetize the pain.

It's easier to mask and hide the pain than get the help we need. *Nobody has time for that. I am too busy for mental and emotional issues. I have people who are counting on me to keep going,* because that's what we preach.

And we continue suffering in silence. This suffering in leadership is all too common because leaders of ministry are often the last ones to get the help they need. We are so busy making sure everyone else is okay and neglect the very care that we ourselves need. There is a fine line we walk as ministers of the gospel. Christ was human and divine. The human side of Him needed the companionship of the disciples when He went to pray. His humanness caused sweat to form as drops of blood when asking God to remove the crucifixion cup from Him.

Don't discount your humanity. I know the Apostle Paul said, "I have become all things to all men, that by all means I might win some" (1 Corinthians 9:22), but you can't do that if you are dead, or sick somewhere in an institution, and can't do what God has asked you to do.

My issues led me into yet another dysfunctional relationship with a woman who I know didn't really care about me, but at the time I couldn't see it. She allowed me to do whatever I wanted to do, and never questioned it. Wow, I thought I had found "the one." I didn't realize I was unhealthy, overweight, and seriously out of shape, speeding my way to an early grave because unchecked, an addiction can take you out. Anyone who really cares about you will not stand by and watch you self-destruct. This is why it is important to have people around you from whom you can receive the truth.

Notice I said, "you can receive." Anyone can tell you the truth, but the human nature will only accept it from sources we trust. Therefore, isolation is one of the tactics the enemy uses to keep believers bound. Without some semblance of spiritual accountability, the enemy can steer and direct you into places you never would have gone freely. I heard it said like this once: "The enemy will take you further than you want you go and keep you longer than you want to stay." This is the secret struggle that I'm talking about.

Dark days were ahead. I found myself blundering through life at this point, dazed and confused. There are still some months that I don't quite remember because I went through them high and drunk. Nothing made sense to me. I felt like people were trying to kill me. I thought this woman I was with had poisoned me.

If you are from the South, you probably have heard about "roots." Roots is a form of witchcraft that came with the slaves from Africa. I thought she had put roots on me, which works on the minds of the weak. I was paranoid, I was accusatory, suffering fits of rage, and jealousy, and at times could become suicidal, but I could not stop myself. These are things most people don't get to see when people are dealing with mental or emotional issues.

I didn't know it at the time, but I was suffering an emotional breakdown. There are men and women of God in the pulpit, preaching and teaching on Sunday morning, who just had a mental meltdown the week prior, but they are back on post like clockwork, still **Blessed and Broken**! These meltdowns don't show up all the time. They are extremely hard to spot by those on the outside, but those who know them best carry the burden with them.

I have discovered that meltdowns have a signature. There are ways to tell if you are about to go into a meltdown. We will discuss this later in the book, figuring out what your triggers are. I liken this process to driving a car and the brakes are squeaking. You hear the brakes making noise, so you roll up the window and turn up the radio so you can't hear them squeaking. This is a picture of ministry for many powerful men and women of God. We know something is wrong, but we ignore the obvious issues by consuming ourselves with other things (rolling up the window). I mean, it only lasts for a few days or so. Right? No big deal!

# Chapter 6

# Enters The Light

I have chosen to include this chapter in the book to show how my path to a sustainable program started. My twenty-eight-year marriage with my spouse is not the norm. Many of us who suffer with mental and emotional issues find it hard to maintain long-lasting relationships. Due to the debilitating nature of mental and emotional issues, it is only right to be honest with those you love. Any person you are considering partnering with in a committed relationship needs to know if you are dealing with these types of issues. Give them the choice to deal with you or not. Not being honest about your **known** issues can severely affect a relationship, because once you are into the relationship, family, friends, and your emotions are involved.

I had started working a temporary assignment with the hopes of getting on permanently with a larger company. The assignment was only supposed to be for a short while, but extended to a full year, and at the end of that year I got hired permanently. I had been working in the operations area processing insurance payments for a major insurance company. My department was next to the mail staging area, which worked well with operations as we got our payments to process more quickly.

I remember sitting at my desk one morning, and I heard a voice I had not heard before. I looked over the median wall that separated the two departments, and saw a tall, light-skinned, beautiful sister working in the mail area. Come to find out she was a temporary worker, and she was single. I watched her from afar. I found out her name by asking one of her coworkers over there. I could not bring myself to talk to her, as yet though. Surely a woman as fine as this would not be interested in a guy like me.

I noticed a young bother would come around to talk to her, and so I assumed he was on game and just left it at that. I didn't like him at first, although I didn't even know him. He was one of those light-skinned brothers with the curly hair that all the ladies loved at the time. You know, one of those R & B singers looking type guys. I asked a co-worker one day who "Al B. Sure" was. She told me "Al B." was a Claims Adjustor there and he and the young lady (who would soon become my fiancé) were just friends. In fact, he was already engaged to be married. What's so funny about this is that we eventually became good friends. He was one of my groomsmen in our wedding.

I told one of her co-workers, "I am going to marry that girl in your department." Call me a stalker if you want to, but I knew in my heart she was the one. I promise you, when you meet the right one, you will know it! There will be no doubt! I mustered enough courage to write her a note and asked her for her number. I didn't know anything about talking to a sophisticated lady like this. So, on the note I did what I knew to do. I said, "Would you go out with me? Check yes or no."

I know you are thinking that was so corny! And you're right! But she must have thought it was cute, as she checked "yes" on the note. She and I started dating secretly because we were both temporary employees and didn't want to sabotage our full-time employment chances at the company. There were many on the job who were under the impression for some reason that I was gay. This was the secret joke around the job. I didn't know why so many people would stare at me. I thought it was because I was tall. When you are tall, people routinely look at you, so I didn't think anything about it.

With the rumor mill in that place, we knew that we would not be able to keep our impending nuptials a secret for long, so I decided to find a job at another insurance company. After my full-time stint with a reputable insurance company, it was easy to find another job. I didn't even have to go through a temporary agency. Many thought it was admirable that she and I did not want to violate our company's nepotism policy which did not make concessions for marriage between individuals in the same department areas. But once I gave my notice to the company, we told everybody we were engaged and getting married. Obviously, the guys in the fleet maintenance area did not get the memo. We were walking to our car in the parking garage, and one of the fleet attendants saw us walking and holding hands, and yelled out across the parking garage to ask her, "Why are you messing with that sissy? You got a real man right here!" We both laughed and told him we were getting married and had been keeping it a secret. He was so embarrassed. Is it possible they were picking up on some of my past issues? Probably so!

My wife was the light I needed to become the man I believe God had always intended for me to be. She convinced me to go back to church, and to get back to using my gifts for the Lord. We started a gospel singing group together and we were able to get some recognition on the local level. We were able to tour, and our group opened for gospel music artists like Kurt Carr and Virtue. We released an independent gospel CD album on our own independent label, and in doing so got invited to sing on the Bobby Jones Gospel Hour, a nationally syndicated gospel television program. She was there to support me with every endeavor. I had never known anyone who really loved and cared about me like that.

Everything was going very well at that time. And again, I started with the self-destructive patterns and derailed the progress we were making. It was not the "what" that I should have been focusing on, but the "why?" Why is it that every time things really start going good, something always happens with me that causes it to fall apart?

My passion for what I was doing was gone. I couldn't see. My vision for what I was doing was gone. I didn't understand what I was doing, and why I was doing it. These were the signs of emotional issues coming to bear.

No one ever says anything about this kind of stuff. For the most part I was all right, but this confusion could last for weeks at a time. I have walked off incredibly good jobs for no other reason than I just didn't want to do it anymore, so inconsistency can be a key indicator of mental or emotional issues.

Now, bear in mind that you may know someone right now who has some of the same tendencies I have mentioned in varying degrees, and prior to reading this you may have thought like me, and just chalked it up to, "That's just the way they are," and chose not to trust them with anything important.

I would spend those days sleeping on the couch, looking for a new job or not. The clouds would eventually move away, the sun would come out again, and I would start a new job. I was back and focused. The newness of the job was what I really liked. Maybe I just needed something new to keep me focused. So, my pattern became starting new projects whenever I felt bored with what I was doing before. I know we might think that's okay, but usually my "experiments" cost me quite a bit of money. I have literally spent thousands of dollars buying expensive music equipment, taking classes in real estate appraising, but never really did anything with the information I had learned.

In retrospect, this is the part that can be so unfair to your unknowing spouse. Now in my case, my issues became known to my wife and me at the same time. We both were learning how to deal with me in those breakdown moments. I don't know if every person is strong enough to deal with all of life's competing issues and your issues too. If a successful relationship is something you desire, then honesty and a maintenance program will need to be a constant reality for you.

Every relationship requires work. Couple that with your own competing issues, and patterns of consistency and accountability are necessary to make that relationship prosper. The good thing that came from all those failed pursuits is the vast knowledge I have gained, and I pass that knowledge along in ministry.

# Chapter 7

# The Ride

*God Spoils The Milk To Make The Baby Get Off The Bottle*

By this time, my wife and I had been married a few years. We had found a good church home and we were active in the community. I had begun to show signs of sustained stability. I was overcoming the self-sabotage patterns that had plagued me for so many years. I finally acknowledged my call and said yes to God. I was enrolled in ministry school and actively pursuing my call.

So here, I want us to recognize there is a correlation between our mental stability and consistency in our spiritual walk.

After working my way into corporate management, I had finally gotten the message. There was no way above the glass ceiling that had been placed over me. I had experienced what many young, educated African American men and women have discovered: there is no place at the top for people who look like me unless

I start my own business. I had become increasingly dissatisfied with my status. Everything was perfect, though. My wife and I were both making great salaries. We had bought a home, we had just had our first child together, everything was wonderful. Yet there was this gnawing feeling on the inside of me that there was more out there for me.

At this point enters my business and spiritual mentor. He was a brother I had met at our local church. I had not met him personally prior to our encounter outside of church, but as I understood it, he had been there for a few months. I just happened to run into him at a fellow church member's printing business as he was leaving, so this brother and I struck up a conversation. During the conversation, I noticed he had a certain way about him. It was not necessarily the way he dressed, but it was something about the way he carried himself.

He had a very wealthy demeanor. When he spoke, I could tell he was the one in charge. The confidence and assurance that he had, the confidence evident in his voice, prompted me to stop him mid-sentence, and ask him, "Brother, what do you do for a living?"

He told me he was the owner and president of an insurance marketing organization. He explained what he did. Simply put, he sold benefits and insurance to local schoolteachers, and in doing so he got paid. I could tell he was making good money. I just didn't know how much.

He invited me to ride along with him on a few of his client appointments, just to get an idea of what his day was like. I took a vacation day from work, and we started about 8:00am and went to several schools. We met with some of his existing clients, and I watched him write a few new clients, as some of his current clients would refer their friends.

When I got home that evening, I was so tired I fell asleep on the couch in full dress. My wife tried to take off my shoes, but my feet were hurting so bad, I told her sleepily, "Please, don't touch my feet."

This was it! The thing I was looking for. Something new and exciting. As per my usual, I jumped into it headfirst without understanding all the details. For example: when you are an independent insurance agent, you don't get paid unless you make sales. I left my job as an operations coordinator for a Fortune 500 insurance company, making a high five-figure salary (which back in 2004-2005 was a good salary) to go full-time commission-only.

Who does that anyway? Let me see.......This guy!

Over the next few months, I learned the grind of the insurance and financial sales industry by walking with my mentor. I spent the better part of my first couple of weeks convincing myself I was not a salesperson. Due to the negative connotation that comes with being a salesperson, I just did not want to associate myself with that stigma. This in turn affected my ability to sell to anyone, including myself. I would not even invest in my own sales pitch, but I kept on taking "The Ride" with my mentor every day for about a year.

It finally came to a head one morning on the way to our office in Columbus, Georgia. The ride was about an hour-and-a-half from Atlanta. We had a very heated conversation because I was not making the money my mentor promised I could make. I was done, and I wanted to go home. The truth was that the pressure had become too much, and at that moment I was having an emotional breakdown, and no one outside of my wife had seen me like this before.

I was willing to get out of the car and walk or find another way back home. Of course, he did not give me what I wanted. He would not allow me to quit on God, myself, or my family, because that was what was coming next, based upon my history. We sat outside our first school appointment of the day discussing my unfortunate unwillingness to go into the school.

My mentor told me, "You are a man of God, but the way you're acting doesn't make you look like one." He gave me some of the best advice I could have ever gotten, but it also came at the price of a blistering scolding. He said, "I always see you out here praying with people, and prophesying and ministering to people. I can see God working through you mightily, but understand this: the same word that will deliver them will also deliver your own household!"

In other words, it was time to stop *acting* like I was a man of God, and it was time to *become* the man of God I was created to be. He tore down the facade I had built and learned to keep up so well. In that very moment, I was for the first time "naked before God." He used a mentor to expose an area in my life He had been trying to get to for quite some time, but I would not allow Him. You see, the ride was not about selling insurance, it was not about becoming the greatest salesperson the industry had ever seen, or even making loads of money. God used the ride to reveal to me the areas in my life that would continue to hold me back from the greater successes He had for me.

The intimacy of the ride allowed my mentor to see and speak to the issues with which I was dealing. This could only happen if there was a connection and time spent working together. Most of us will not receive words of correction from people we do not trust.

There are leaders who have been stuck at this crossroad for many years. I had learned to settle for the façade of being great, but inwardly I was an empty shell. I knew how to look good and talk good, and speak the "church lingo," but I had the hardest time believing for myself. I could believe so strongly for other people, but when it came to my own beliefs, I was walking around blind, leading the blind.

This was the day that changed everything for me, in my sales career, my church responsibility, and my home.

I wiped my eyes after that blistering scolding from my mentor. I stayed behind as he went into the school. I made a deal with God that I was going to continue this time in what I started, but I needed His help, because I didn't know how to finish anything.

When I entered the school that day, there was something different in the atmosphere I knew I was in the right place at the right time. It was a Kairos moment with me and God. There was such an anointing on me when I entered that school, one that I had never experienced before. I drew people like I had never experienced before in ministry. I wrote policies on all the unenrolled teachers at the school. Even individuals who would not write with my mentor wrote with me. From that moment on, I experienced that same favor of God in every transaction.

In that instant, God transformed my mind about who I was to Him. Everywhere I went, people began to ask me if I was a pastor. I replied, "No, I just play one on television." LOL! But what I did not understand was that I had taken a step over into destiny and God was confirming what He was doing in my life. It was not about selling insurance, but making sure that all people could experience the joy of being in the moment with Him.

As you will read in the next chapter, the Jesus model for discipleship is one of the most misunderstood and under-utilized tools in the body of Christ. There are those who do not subscribe to the provision that God has provided to us in His word. However, these systems in place currently weigh heavily upon the spiritual hearing and understanding of the person who is leading. There are powerful leaders in the body of Christ who never come to the pinnacle of what God had prepared for them because they are looking for confirmation from man rather than from God. So, the time I spent in the insurance industry was about learning who I was in God by way of the "Discipleship Model."

My path became much clearer for me. I had a plan to get the things God had shown me. Surely this "insurance thing," as I called it, was the way God had always intended to provide me with the resources to take us to the next level. Even in ministry I had begun to see promotion. I was an armor bearer to the pastor. I was teaching in the school of ministry and Sunday school. I was seeing people saved and restored because this was one of the things my mentor stressed.

This thing is about seeing people saved, the money is just a byproduct. My mentor was gifted in many spiritual gifts, but evangelism seemed natural for him. Sure, we all need money to live, but it is important to *give back*. We would pray for teachers and their marriages. We would hold Bible studies for those who were interested. Ministry became my focus, not the money, and the money came. Boy, did it come! For the first time in my life, I was doing exactly what I was supposed to be doing in ministry, and it didn't get old to me. Sharing the gospel was always new and fresh. God was revealing new truths to me. Man, was it an exciting time.

I found a stability in ministry that I had not found in anything else in my life. I told my mentor that our experiences were the stuff of legend, and I was going to author a book one day, and "The Ride" would be one of the chapters. I must tell you, being able to travel and shop and the freedom to work my own schedule kept me going in the sales game, but it was only a temporary stop for me. I have learned that we must transition, as the Bible calls it moving "from glory to glory." (2 Corinthians 3:18) Sometimes when things are going well, we don't want to move on from that place. I had fallen into that trap where everything was good, it was comfortable, and I was content with exactly the way it was.

There is a saying that I have coined when it comes to God getting us to move on to the next level. *God spoils the milk to make the baby get off the bottle.* My time at our current ministry was sweet, but it had to end. I heard God say it loud and clear.

Now, I did what most young ministers would do, I talked to my pastor to get his advice on what I heard God saying. I did what I should have done by letting leadership know, and received some valuable wisdom, but my job was still to obey what God said! When your time is up, God will use what I call the "Misunderstanding Test" to wound you for the purposes of getting you to let go of the familiar and comfortable. In other words, He will make the familiar look very unfriendly and unfamiliar to you, and the comfortable very unbearable.

Progress in ministry comes at the expense of comfort. We see many stories of people of God who are extremely blessed, but the question in my mind is: What did it cost them to get it? Everything in God is going to cost us something. Every covenant that God made with man required a sacrifice. My friend, if you are in ministry, then you are that sacrifice. Surprise! God used my time in the insurance sales arena to reveal weaknesses in my character. These are sometimes the hardest areas in themselves for leaders to see. I have learned it is the character weaknesses that come back to find you when success is at hand. Some of the trouble we are seeing in leadership today in the body of Christ has to do with character issues, not mental or emotional ones. Amen!

I know the subject matter of this book is about the mental and emotional challenges that leaders face, but I would be remiss if I did not mention that character thing as well. The additional skills I learned from being an entrepreneur are the same skills and traits I use every single day in ministry: perseverance, tenacity, passion, and compassion. I have learned how to overcome my fears. I saw the word that I was teaching to everybody else starting to take effect in my own life. This has always been a part of God's plan for maturing

His ministry gifts. "The Discipleship Model" is God-inspired and will not fail the leader once you have been successfully discipled. I liken this model to advanced military training, because you submit yourself to another's ability to bring the best out of you.

You go in with the understanding in mind, "This is to mature me, and everything I endure will serve to stabilize me in ministry." This encounter must be from the view of a military strategist. God has a plan for you and me and wants to bring that plan to fruition in the Earth. This will only happen one way, and that's His way!

# Chapter 8

# The Discipleship Model

### *Broken Shepherds Produce Broken Sheep*

Over the years in ministry, I have had the opportunity to walk with some powerful and anointed up-and-coming leaders in the body of Christ. One area of need for many of these young, called, gifted, and anointed vessels is proper discipleship. There are no skipping steps in God's process. The church may see your gifts and promote you, but that's not necessarily how God works. The "giftings and callings are without repentance" (Romans 11:29), so you can be a powerful, anointed, and charismatic leader and still be lacking in some spiritual areas because of a lack of discipleship. When you have had early success in ministry, it's hard to see the need for mentorship. It would be hard for any leader to go back and submit to another man's leadership after having major success in ministry. Part of the discipleship process deals with that very thing, that pride. As the Bible has warned us, "pride goes before destruction" (Proverbs 16:18) and pride is a character trait we usually cannot see in ourselves. Pride in leadership may manifest itself in many ways. It can be something as simple as not being able to work with other ministries outside of your ministerial understanding or comfort zone. Just because they don't do it like you do it doesn't mean it's not of God.

For non-leadership believers, this may manifest in a lack of consistency in their walk, whatever the issues are. Discipleship was designed to root out those things we keep well-hidden. How is this related to mental/emotional issues, you ask? Many who know they have issues have learned how to hide them well or deny there are any issues at all, behaviors that are rooted in pride and self-righteousness.

When confronted about questionable behaviors or inconsistency, some may respond, "God speaks to me, and He would tell me if it were was an issue!" Maybe God is telling someone else to tell them because they do not hear Him because of that pride. So, the discipleship model roots out any source of pride, bitterness, or weakness there may be. But this is not the model many of us know about. Some of us were given a religious model and were told, "This is the only way God does things, and anyone who does not agree with us is wrong."

Our second ministry plant started in our living room: "Kingdom Empowerment Center Ministries."

We had just left Hebron World Church, a pioneering work in Covington, Georgia, where my wife and I were foundational pastors. My family was in turmoil because of how our departure unfolded. As you already know, I had left my good corporate job. I was in sales and making some money. It seemed like an exciting time to start a ministry. God had already called me to start, but I had chosen other alternatives before then, because I did not feel "I" was ready for the call yet. One of the major benefits to walking closely with a lead pastor in a church plant is you get to see them before they have been polished.

When it comes to mentoring, remember that: *the leaders we are today; are not the leaders we have always been.* There are things that were perfected in you by trial and error. I was able to see my friend and pastor make several mistakes that hurt the ministry. I gained valuable wisdom, even though I was there in disobedience. God never told me to go there. It was a good opportunity, but it still wasn't what He called me to do. Hence the family turmoil that I talked about a minute ago.

The first year of K.E.C.M. was disappointing, to say the least. When you start ministry, everybody tells you they are with you and they will support you. But I have learned there is a significant difference between those who are *with* you, and those who are *for* you. It will not be hard to find those who are for you if you have been walking in integrity in ministry. Finding those who are with you, that's a whole different ball game. I routinely preached to empty chairs. Some of the most powerful sermons were never heard by anyone but me and God.

I didn't understand why, but God was dealing with my perceived understanding of ministry. I remember crying one night in prayer and telling God, "I know that the ministry isn't going so well, and I know it's because I left the ministry that trained me without the pastor's blessing." I had never heard God before as clearly as at that moment. He said, "Who told you that was My way?" Meaning: when did earthly authority trump heavenly authority? After that first year, the ministry grew out of the house, and we moved into our own location.

Once again with everything going well, and experiencing God moving in the ministry, "me" got in the way!

The people pleaser pastor, following the voice of the people rather than the voice of God, allowed us to overcommit financially to a facility we could not afford, based upon the word of ministry leaders who said they were "with" us. This dealt a serious financial blow to the ministry as we invested heavily in renovating the property. Outside of my own issues, this was my first real encounter with leaders dealing with mental and emotional issues too. In retrospect I think they made the financial commitment with honest intentions, but that mental and emotional thing came knocking as the pressures of ministry increased. Why hadn't anyone seen these behaviors before? My inability to properly discern their mental state allowed me to put them into leadership positions within the ministry. I expected leaders to be consistent and to have already worked out some of their basic issues with God. I had never encountered leaders who struggled with mental and emotional issues manifesting in drug use and sexual addictions before.

You mean to tell me there are men and women of God who are addicted to drugs and other vices, yet lead powerful ministries? Yes! For me, this would mean going out, sometimes at all times of the night, looking for them. And when I did find them, the usual conversation would have them saying, "Nothing is wrong," even though it was obvious they were high. Their patterns of inconsistency had stayed hidden because they had not walked with anyone closely enough to recognize and address the concerns and their families had covered "their nakedness."

This was an immature and novice mistake on my part because of my own lack of understanding of just how prevalent mental health issues are in the church today. Some of the most dependable leaders we had serving with us throughout the years in ministry dealt with mental or emotional issues, which sometimes manifested into disappearing or checkouts at the most inopportune times. The pressure of the moment caused them to shrink back or find a way not to take on greater responsibilities. I want to make this point abundantly clear here: I don't believe there is anything wrong with having leaders who know and **effectively** manage their mental and emotional issues. It's the ones who don't manage their symptoms well and continually self-destruct and expect everyone else to allow them to continue in this manner without some type of accountability. There are churches started every week by gifted ministers dealing with mental or emotional issues, who need to be submitted under authority. However, being submitted requires accountability, so it's much easier to just start a work. These leaders are dynamic, and have a drawing for people, but the challenge comes when their issues start to become a problem. The ministries fold, with the people paying the ultimate price.

There are those who have been turned away from the body of Christ because of the treatment they receive from leaders with unrecognized mental or emotional issues. I am all for pastoral health and wellness! If you are a pastor and you are so busy that you cannot stay in contact with leaders within your ministry, then you are too busy and are subject to finding yourself on the wrong side of a hospital bed. I received training and ministry mentorship in operational matters, like: What do you do when the people aren't tithing like they should? How do you pay the rent during the seasonal slumps? I was also given a solid foundation on spiritual matters, but no one ever told me about how many people there were in the body struggling with their mental and emotional health.

So, what do you do when you realize you have leaders struggling with their own mental or emotional health? Now we are getting into the significant issues here. Are you starting to get the answers to so many of the questions you may have had? Why did they just up and leave and not say anything? What did we do to them to make them leave the church like that? No call. They just up and disappeared. These are people you ate with, served with, sometimes for years, and had not recognized the issues they had. They were allowed to limp on because they had been such an important part of the ministry. Try explaining to your youth ministry why their youth pastor suddenly just up and quit on them and didn't tell them why. For us, this was a real scenario that affected our ministry in negative ways because these leaders often had good influence with the people.

So, the truth is that no one did anything to them. This was just an outpouring of unchecked mental and emotional issues. I am certain there are those who have been hurt by me in ministry because I just did not know how my issues were affecting my leadership decisions. Many of the mistakes I made in ministry would never have happened had I been fully submitted to the discipleship process, which is a powerful tool in the hands of God to root out the things that are hidden.

Every believer must come to the place of revelation that to fill up on Christ means we choose to let go of all the other things that had us bound. Easier said than done, you say? I agree, but our Father made a way for us to be able to successfully navigate the issues that affect us all. Do not be fooled. We have all been influenced by the world we have been brought up in.

This is the reason discipleship is necessary: *You cannot become what you have never seen before. You can never grow beyond your exposure!* The discipleship model is a way to show young and maturing believers how to navigate the traps of this life. But before someone can disciple another, the question that must be answered is: "Has the one discipling gone through the process of being discipled?" Make no mistake, a seed reproduces after its own kind. Whatever issues, problems, and insecurities the mentor has will affect the mentee. *Broken shepherds produce broken sheep.* If you don't believe me, just hold a striped stick in front of a pregnant sheep and see if the babies come out spotted. (Genesis 30:38-39)

Some of the hurts believers experience in "church" are because of immature leadership. As stated earlier, there are many young ministries that start every week due to a perceived offense. But the place of offense is only the beginning of discipleship, not the beginning stages of ministry, as many have assumed.

One of the methods God has always intended for us to use to assist the body of Christ in the growth process is the discipleship model. Within this model there are many tools He uses to help us identify where we are "not." Everybody can tell you where they are, but the discovery of where we are *not* leads to maturation. We are talking about this model because this process will identify hidden mental or emotional weaknesses that should be addressed:

**Growth Methods:**

- **The Misunderstanding Test**
- **Intimacy with Jesus**
- **Mentoring Relationships/Discipleship**
- **Deliverance**
- **Duplication**
- **Elevation**

One of the first tests every leader must go through is called the Misunderstanding Test, which is part of the discipleship model. The weapons of God are both offensive and defensive in nature. Discipleship is an offensive weapon that God uses to mature His believers. You don't really know who a person is until they have been offended. The offense reveals emotional weaknesses. When we are angry or hurt over a perceived wrong, we often feel as though we have the right to respond in the way we want to respond. God is using these instances to show us our character flaws.

Every believer is offended purposely by God in some way to mature us. The offense is something like chastening. According to the word of God, "He chastens those He loves." (Hebrews 12:6) So, count it all joy, because if God did not love us, He would not take the time to chasten us! Stop running from offenses. People who offend you are your friends, whether you know it or not. Most people never look at themselves or ask the question, "Why does what they do offend me so?" See, you can't mature until you can answer this question for yourself.

God has already given us the strategy for growing believers, not buildings, but we have discounted its effectiveness because worldly methods work faster than the traditional or old-school methods, as some have called them. What this really means is submitting to the process the way God has designed it, to get the desired effect. God often will use the offense to reveal what is truly in a person's heart. Therefore, the discipleship model is so important to the growth and maturation of believers. The mentor will point out to you the things that God is working on in your life. I promise you! You will not always like what a mentor has to say, but if they don't offend you then you are not growing.

I have wounded many people of God during the process of them walking with me, but it is a necessary tool for rooting out pride, bitterness, self-loathing, inferiority issues, and many other things we have become crafty at hiding from everyone else. Yet God sees it all! In many church circles there are young ministers who have learned the culture, and how to speak the "lingo," but the anointing on a person's life will show up when a leader's private life begins to match the public life. The private life of a leader is just as important as the public image. For the believer, the public view/image comes out of a commitment to the concepts/precepts found in the word of God!

Make no mistake, there is a tangible presence a spiritual leader can detect in your life when you have made the transition from just being a public leader and have become a leader at home, which is our first ministry. Far too often, we have powerful leaders in the pulpit, but the home life does not resemble what they are preaching. Gone are the days where we do not live at home what we are preaching in the pulpit. And the amen goes right there!

When you as a leader in training have been wounded by those who have been called to mature you, this is a natural part of the maturation process. The wound signifies you are a "son." I dare say there are quite a few who did not stay and stand to learn the very first lesson of discipleship. When I was wounded, I did not stay. I ran and did not capture all the principles of the lesson.

## The Misunderstanding Test

The misunderstanding test exposes the true nature of your intent. The offense will often bring on justification, and the internal reasoning that they were wrong for "doing that to me." It begins to expose the rebellious nature of a leader that, if unchecked, will create more rebellious leaders. When offended with the misunderstanding test, it tests the expectations we have for and about others. *How could they do this to me? I have been serving, tithing, and doing everything I have been asked to do. They know me, how can they treat me like this?* When you think you are something, then offenses seem wrong to you.

Consider this: *dead men don't make a sound.* This is where God is taking us in this process, the place where we die to our perceived rights because we are servants of God. There are thousands of people of God who are doing other things and justifying and calling it ministry because they don't have to submit to anyone. Being a servant of God means we serve His people! The discipleship model helps us to die to ourselves.

When we are at the place where we don't care if anyone knows our name, if no one ever says how powerful the message we preached was, or how great our singing was, and we are okay with that, then we are maturing according to God's plan for us.

When leaders come to our ministry from other places, we routinely ask them to come in as "no names." Meaning we don't call them any title, we let the people see them serve, and the people will identify who they are.

We don't have to call them anything. When the people see them serving, they will call them what they are.

When I look at the story of Moses, his trip to the back side of the desert was about removing Egypt from him. God must remove Egypt from us, too, because not doing so will always cause us to desire what was easiest for us. Even the children of Israel, although they had been delivered from Egypt, still had a desire to go back there because it was easier than their current circumstances. No one in their right mind says, "I want suffering and pain to be my portion!" So how does God get Egypt out of us?

**Intimacy With Jesus**

Intimacy with Jesus caused the great growth for the early apostles. It is the "come and I will make you" (Matthew 14:19), part that we may take for granted as spiritual leaders. I tell all leaders: *there is a time to walk with our mentors, but then there is a time when we walk alone with Jesus*. What that looks like for each person will be different. We cannot make ourselves into what God is called for without intimacy with Christ. The purpose of the disciples following Jesus was to get out of them what the world had already put in them. Some issues we deal with, God does not reveal to our mentors. These are things He deals with directly.

Remember, there will be a time where Christ will call us away to our mountaintop and valley low experiences. In those moments with Him, we discover who we really are. I have heard some call it "the dark night of the soul." For me, it was my Midian experience. It's that place where we can't hear or see spiritually, and we must find our anchor in what we believe. A faith that cannot be tested, cannot be trusted! If it were not so, then there would be no need for the 23rd Psalm. This is a picture of intimacy with the great Shepherd. Jesus will lead us in the path God has for us.

The reason many leaders in the body of Christ are limited is because our greatest intimacy times were with our earthly mentors. How can you *reproduce something you have never seen before*? If God has called you to birth something unique in the earth, you will not get the full picture looking at the partial pictures you have always seen. If you were like me, you went into ministry with no idea what ministry meant. I was just young and full of zeal, but not according to knowledge. I submitted to the process of becoming the man of God that He called me to be at the direction of others. They were already successful in ministry, so they knew exactly what I needed to obtain the successes they had. So, we become perfect copies of our mentors.

But what God is looking for is the unique you *He created*. If you are mentoring others, make sure they look like Christ and not you. We already have you, and it was enough when God created you. If not, He would have created more of you on His own. Let's make sure your mentees look like Jesus when it's all said and done!

## Mentoring Relationships/Discipleship

Mentorship was the beginning of understanding for me. I had always wondered why things routinely failed with me, but I never had anyone I could trust to show me. My mentor pointed out areas of inconsistency in my walk and in my life. He was there when I went through my meltdown process.

Mentoring relationships are a foundational component of a believer's success. But before we get into the specifics of the mentoring relationships, I want to discuss the term *fatherhood*. I am the father of three sons, and this has taught me many valuable lessons to employ as I am leading others spiritually. Mentoring is temporary, but fatherhood is for a lifetime. In many church circles, I have heard many powerful men and women being referred to as a spiritual father or mother. I have learned that being a true spiritual parent has to do with how you employ the authority and the resources you have to create successes for those you lead. When my second eldest son started his third year in college in Arkansas, I wanted him to have transportation to go back to school. He had proven over the previous two years that he could handle more responsibility. As a father, my job, just as it was for King David, was to prepare for the future needs and successes of my sons.

My own mentor referred to his mentor in ministry as a father. His own spiritual father sent him a check once. When he asked him why he sent the check, his response was, "Because you needed it." Now that's a father! If I am a true spiritual father or mother, it then becomes my responsibility to support the ministries I have "birthed," or those I have taken on the responsibility to lead.

My eldest son has been married several years now, and by the time this book hits the market I will be a grandfather. When I have not heard or talked to him in a couple of weeks, an alarm starts to go off in my head: "I have not heard from my son." I pick up the phone to call him and say, "Hey big guy, is everything good?" That is a true picture of fatherhood.

We must be careful as those who are called to be spiritual parents that we don't have so many "children" we get the Old Woman Who Lived in a Shoe syndrome: we have so many kids, we don't know what to do! If we are too busy with all our kids, one of them may get left out or forgotten. You can't be a spiritual parent to those you do not know. Just because they join your network and pay a fee does not make you a spiritual parent. If you don't even know the name of their ministry, you are not their spiritual parent, you are a mentor, and guess what? That's ok too; you are still needed and necessary to the growth of the body!

Additionally, when mentoring people who have been hurt and marginalized by people who were mothers and father to them, it's hard to consider a ministry leader as a mother or father. If I am training leaders in my ministry, which we do, and another ministry that is tied to us has a need for a leader, guess what? Those leaders I'm training will go and assist that ministry in whatever capacity is necessary as part of their training. Some of my greatest leadership lessons came from walking with the pastor of a new church plant. How dare we call ourselves spiritual parents, with thirty ministers sitting on our front row dressed to the nines, but our "spiritual children" need just one to assist with something as simple as covering for a Sunday, so that they could have some off time? Remember, *not everyone is in ministry full time.*

So, what should we be looking for in a mentoring relationship? First, a mentor must be secure and proven in who they are. They will be unable to mentor you properly if they are dealing with what I call "gift envy." This is when a mentor has been gifted but lacks maturity. This type of mentor will never allow you to move beyond where they have stopped, in terms of growth. Ask King Saul about that one! Do not be fooled: just because someone has a large ministry does not mean they are the perfect mentor, or they have the time necessary to disciple the way the Bible has prescribed for you.

Next, the relationship must be more than the occasional phone conversation. I call these long-distance relationships, which to me have less accountability than direct mentorship. I have tried to mentor long distance, but it doesn't always give the mentee what they need. Some things are taught, others are caught. I routinely require that a mentee walk closely with me on a weekly basis, so they get to see me in the good times as well as the bad. They and their families will have dinner with my family, because you can only hide your family dysfunction for so long. Mentees will eventually see it if they are walking closely with their mentors. People don't do what's expected, they do what's inspected. Unless they are the senior leaders of a ministry, this may cause conflict with their perceived loyalty to their current ministry.

A mentor's job is not to be your friend. Now if you become friends through the process, then that's a bonus. As you read in an earlier chapter, "The Ride," our fight came due to my current emotional status. I was ready to quit like always, and no one could convince me otherwise. He walked with me through my issues and never judged me for it. In fact, my mentor was keen on balance in five key areas of life: Mental, Physical, Emotional, Family, and Financial. So, this was a requirement for me every day. I had to do something in each one of those areas daily. This was the beginning of a regimen that would help bring stability to my life. Additionally, a difference of ministry philosophies could eventually result in a clash and cause problems, which is not something we should allow to happen. If they can't walk fully with you, then they are probably not the mentee God has sent you. When Jesus called His first disciples, they had to leave the familiar and follow this new direction.

If God has called for a particular mentor for you, it is your responsibility to move into position. Your mentor will begin to point out your areas where you are lacking.

As a reminder for those who are mentoring others, I encourage you not to fall into the mentorship trap of having fifty to sixty so-called mentees in ministry. You will not have enough spiritual capacity within you to train them effectively if you are using the Christ discipleship model. I have seen this model in the body of Christ, and many times it's only about the money you pay these so-called mentoring organizations. Those who contribute the most money are the ones known by their mentors. Jesus had twelve whom He mentored effectively. Now I know the Bible says we will do greater works than He did, but you cannot mentor people whom you don't even know.

I have seen instances where leaders are tied to ministries for mentorship, and the person tasked with mentoring them does not even know their names. Because of the size of the mentor's ministry, it's assumed you will get something by "osmosis." You need intimate contact with your mentor, consistently on a daily or at least weekly basis, if possible.

## Deliverance

Since many of you reading this book are in ministry, I won't go into the spiritual basis for deliverance or the need for deliverance for every believer. Deliverance is a topic that is also taboo in many church circles. But the need for deliverance is necessary, as we all have been born into a world that is not our own and have received an image that does not reflect the glory of Christ. When it comes to deliverance, I have found two parts that are required. There is the denouncing of the things that have had us bound, but the second step is to close doors of opportunity for the enemy to come in. Sometimes this will mean that we will need to confront some of the "demons" that have been a burden to us.

Part of my deliverance came when I mustered the courage to meet my stepfather face-to-face. I forgave him for the things he had done to me, but he didn't even realize he had done anything wrong. What's funny is that he challenged me on the use of the word regarding reconciliation. But the forgiveness was not for him, it was for me.

I found the encounter to be very liberating. The fear that was birthed in me at the hands of my abuser, which had continued to cause me issues well into my adult life as well as my ministry career, was now gone! It is a known fact that the abused tend to also become people pleasers. Being a people pleaser and being a pastor do not mix. My early decisions in ministry were often based upon keeping people happy and coming to the church. My emotions caused me to move off what God called me to do. A mentor would have recognized the issues in me and spoken to them much earlier in my ministry career.

As stated earlier, I have learned to find the flesh in it. Everything God calls for prospers, and if it does not, then there is some flesh mixed in with the way God wants to do it. Deliverance closes those doors that the enemy has access to in our lives. These doors can be natural or spiritual, but both must be addressed in the life of every believer, and especially if we are going to be leading people.

I believe, many times those who suffer with mental and emotional issues must go back and confront the "demons" that haunt them. Ignoring them will no longer work. Interestingly, the recurring nightmares I continued to have into my young adult life ceased after that encounter. That house that I grew up in had haunted my dreams for so many years, and it took me facing my abuser to receive my deliverance.

But what do you do if your abuser is not alive anymore? Write a letter and place it on their grave, or write the letter and then burn it. The most important thing is to *acknowledge* that it is an issue. You will never address what you do not consider a problem.

## Duplication

A container causes everything you put in it to bend to the will or shape of the container. My brothers and sisters, this is called duplication. There can be no duplication without proper impartation. Christ was imparting Himself into the apostles. They learned from being around Him, watching Him, asking Him questions about why He did what He did or said. Far too many relationships require that a mentee be silent and not ask questions. But isn't that what they did in the Bible with Jesus? When Jesus called for His disciples to go out from Him, they were not yet apostles on the inside. You don't become an apostle on the inside without the process of duplication. This process solidifies the training in you.

Let's recap what we have heard so far. First, there is the separation process where God separates you from the misconceptions of what being in His service means. He then uses a mentor to disciple you in the "character traits of Christ." Not themselves. We all are being "transformed into the image of His dear Son." This must always be the pattern used for discipleship. I often tell those I am mentoring, "We don't need another Apostle

Mike. I want to see what God is calling and causing *you* to become!"

I've heard it said that "imitation is the sincerest form of flattery," meaning that when people try to be like you it should be received as a compliment. This couldn't be farther from the truth. We don't need another person like anyone else. God made us uniquely different for a purpose, otherwise we would have all been the same. A mentor's job is to help you discover areas of unrecognized opportunities for growth in you. A mentor is not necessarily your friend, and this should always be kept in mind. It is a bonus when you have a mentor who can also become a friend, but this must not be allowed to distract from the true nature of the relationship. Their job is to better you, not to be your best friend!

This exposure to my mentor helped me to recognize the duality in my own life. When you are isolated, no one really sees what you are. You can only hide who or what you really are for so long. Duplication causes the growth to be solidified. As I have said before, some things are taught, others are caught. When you start to disciple others, you are causing growth for yourself also. If you ever want to learn something, teach it first. This of course is the next step in the Jesus discipleship model. "Come and go out from Me" (Luke 14:24) was how Jesus laid it on the early apostles.

## Elevation

Many strive for elevation in ministry without the process of a proper or an inadequate discipleship model. I have two sayings I tell all leaders who come to walk with me: *We don't promote people here, God does that,* and *we don't make great ministry gifts, that's God's job!* Why is this so important? Because if man can make you, then he can also break you. Many young minsters of the gospel have found themselves operating in other "callings" when they have been called to lead God's sheep, because someone took away the identity given to them. If God gives the identity, no man can take it away from you.

I know that you, like me, have run into some of these gifts working in other fields, and I'll ask them the same question: "What are you doing about your ministry call?" They are despondent, and more times than not they are where they are because someone did not know how to disciple them when they were young in ministry. They often felt that their mentors had turned on them, but as we understand it now, the offense was a part of God's plan all along and they chose not to stay and deal with the lesson of the offense.

To follow God's plan for our maturation means elevation is certain. If we look at everything that was done God's way, there is increase! That is God's plan. He did not go through the trouble of making and molding and shaping you for you to be ordinary! Nobody puts ordinary household items on display. Why? Because everyone has them. Who cares if you put a toaster on display, can it make toast? So, God is in the business of making instruments, not objects to sit on a shelf. Take courage and know that elevation is on the way. If you don't feel that way, the real question you need to be asking is: "Why don't I feel that way?" Usually this is an indicator that there is some flesh in the way that needs to be addressed. If God promotes you, then you are ready for the stage that has been set.

# Chapter 9

# Mental Health as Wealth

*Their Emergency Does Not Have
To Be Your Immediacy*

By now, I'm sure you are wondering, "Where's the blessed part of all of this?" From my perspective, it has all been a blessing because I have seen many who did not make it past this point. The hurts, the secret drug habits, the alcohol, the infidelity, or the depression caused them to leave ministry with only regrets and excuses. The ones I have had the opportunity to talk to after they left ministry all seem to have the same story. Nothing else just seemed to satisfy after that. They still deal with the same issues, they are just not leading a church anymore.

The greatest triumph for me is that I can help others to recognize the starting point of their mental and emotional health issues. I do not believe people are born with mental health issues, aside from being diagnosed with birth defects as a root cause, but we become the byproducts of sin in a broken world.

I remember when I was about ten years old, in elementary school, and I asked my teacher to put a bandage on a wound on my back because I could feel my shirt rubbing on it.

As she lifted my shirt, she gasped and asked, "Who did this to you?"

I reluctantly told her my stepfather had beaten me for not taking out the trash. She asked me how often I got beatings, and I told her, "All the time."

I heard her begin to sob and pray, and she said to me, "I have heard of children who are in terribly situations similar to what you are in, and they have discovered a way to escape the pain of the moment."

My teacher taught me something I used to escape. She said in the story, these children would create a place in their minds and would go there whenever they were getting a beating. This would take away some of the pain. What she was telling me about is what we now know as Dissociative Identity Disorder. I created my own separate personality to shield me from the pain of the moment. I did not know it at the time, but this simple advice caused me to fracture my personality through what I like to call displacement.

You see, "Dwayne," my middle name, is the guy who was always getting into trouble. He was the one who took the punishment for what he had been doing, not me. These types of behaviors can be the beginning of classic multiple personality syndrome. After much research into the matter, this appears to happen under extreme duress. The child feels they have no help and no way out, and create this "friend" who steps in to take the punishment for their wrongs. These so-called friends begin to take on lives of their own, and at times may manifest unannounced. In extreme cases of the disorder, the child may have several personalities that are a support system but operate autonomously.

In my adult life, this manifested in not being able to sustain healthy social or personal relationships, and being unable to sustain consistency in anything I was doing. As stated earlier, there is a long trail of "projects" in my past that never got accomplished. As spiritual leaders, we know the scriptures, but it seems we don't always see that we need them for ourselves.

For instance, the Bible speaks to mental health, but we don't view in that way. In (3 John 1:2), the writer exhorts his listeners with this greeting: "Beloved, I pray that in every way you may prosper and enjoy good health, as your soul also prospers." The soul speaks to the mind, the will, and the emotions, does it not? So, God's plan has always been for us to be whole, the Bible calls it being "complete and lacking nothing." (James 1:4)

Every situation is different, and this process I'm describing is part of my own mental health and stability process. I highly recommend speaking with someone on a regular basis. A checkup or tune up, if you will. I know some may seek the comfort of peer relationships, and there is nothing wrong with that, but sometimes those do not allow you to express how you really feel without condemnation or correction. You need someone who can listen and assess what's going on with you, not just from a spiritual perspective but also from a mental and emotional one as well. There are men of God I have walked with for years, but I never felt like I could be honest with any of them about the struggles with my mental health. I always felt the need to project a strong spiritual image before them. So, I went on suffering and coping with the symptoms the best way I knew how.

As alluded to earlier in the book, I was a secret drinker for a long time. I think I had just learned to hide it well. My biggest "tell" was my weight gain which had increased to over 450 pounds. I kept this fact from my wife because I know she would have been worried. I have always been a big guy, and so many did not recognize what I was dealing with on the inside. I was in the grocery store one afternoon, and I ran into some members of a previous ministry plant.

I could see in their eyes they were concerned about me, but kept it light and cordial. As I walked away, I heard the wife say, "Man, he looks bad," to which her husband replied, "I know!" You see my "slip was showing," but because I was so isolated, no one could tell me. I'm sure what they were seeing were the outward effects of drinking, but I know my countenance and spirit man were dark. The outside is simply a reflection of what is going on with the inside.

I spent ten years away from friends and family. I called it my wilderness experience, but what I was really doing was avoiding my family. My family consists of mostly ministers and leaders in the body of Christ, and I knew they would be able to see me. One person I was particularly avoiding was my Aunt Ellen, a powerful prophet. She was the one who spoke over me when I was younger. Every time I saw her, and I wasn't doing what God has called me to do, she would say, "Nope, that's not it," so I avoided family all together.

I have since gone back and begun to reconcile with my family, but I call that ten-year period my Midian experience. That's the place of intimacy with Christ where He took me to work out issues on the back side of the desert. We will discuss that in detail in the next chapter.

Part of my emotional healing has been going back and talking with my family members about the what and the why. Many on the outside never knew what my sister and I had been facing during our early years. I found resentment in my heart because I wanted someone to rescue us, but they could not discern what was going on. Or if they did, they didn't say anything because my stepfather was a good provider. Facing your emotional traumas is key to your mental and emotional stability. Not carrying the burdens of past wrongs or mistakes goes a long way to bring stability to you.

Confession to God is part of the process, but the Bible also addresses this issue "first the natural and then the spiritual." (1 Corinthians 15:46) So, making amends for wrongs or addressing hurts is a good practice. If I can say this, we are so immature at relationships in the church. Therefore, the body of Christ is disjointed and disconnected. Just because we disagree about something does not mean the relationship must be over. Getting rid of the internal baggage helps us to process every situation in the proper light. There are times when others inadvertently wrong us and we take offense at how they treat us. The hurt and pain in us causes us to process their intent wrongly, and therefore we get the wrong conclusion, choosing to believe "you meant to hurt me," when they just didn't know.

Talking to a professional is a good practice, because you need that unbiased ear to share what you are seeing and understanding. Your spouse may not be the one to give you the best advice all the time about what you are seeing or going through. Their perspective will always be biased because of their love for you. That love will sometimes cause them to not tell you the truth, or they tell you in a way that softens the blow, when what you need is a shot, "straight with no chaser"! The unbiased professional can tell you the truth, and you have a choice to accept what they are saying or continue to walk around in self-denial.

As I said before, I am not here to debate the theological correctness of going for mental counseling. I'm only sharing what has been working for me. This is not an end-all be-all. Some things you find in this book will be helpful, and some useful information you can use to inspire change in your congregations. They may not be of value to you yet, but each person must find their own "recipe" that is exactly right for them. It's our job to walk along with them as they find out what this recipe is.

People, that is called discipleship, which is the first mandate of apostolic ministry: "making disciples of all people." (Matthew 28:19) The beautiful thing is your strategy doesn't have to look like anyone else's strategy. You really don't have to discuss your process with anyone unless you want to. I encourage you to just let those around you see the changes and the difference in you. When we stop talking about getting better and start displaying behaviors that say we want to be better, then we will get the support we need from those around us.

The reality is that we have no control over this thing. My friend, you are riding a horse and this thing has a mind of its own, and it's taking you for a ride through the countryside. So, any steps we take to bring balance to our mental and emotional selves is about bringing that Sabbath Rest peace that the Bible talks about. (Hebrews 4:9) To do that, we must follow the pattern that Christ has set to restore His glorious image to the church.

Here is a simple list of daily practical things that I, as a leader, have incorporated into my busy day for maintaining my mental and emotional health.

Some of these apply to those in ministry, but anyone can benefit from a mental health routine. This is not an exhaustive list, but it does address many of the areas that **<u>can</u>** be triggers for most:

**My Keys to Maintaining Mental/Emotional Stability:**

- **Daily Exercise/Healthier meal choices/ Drink lots of water!**
- **Massages/Manicures/Pedicures (Treat yourself)**
- **"No Church stuff" days off (We do not talk shop!)**
- **Periodical Mental Counseling sessions**
- **Daily/Weekly accountability with mentoring/peer relationships**
- **Let others help carry the load. You can't do it alone! (Train others to do the work with you!)**
- **If possible, work shorter hours on teaching nights, if bi-vocational**

- **Limit social media time/access (No devices at the dinner table!)**
- **Set boundaries! *Their emergency does not have to be your immediacy*!**

**I left a little space at the bottom of this page for you to add some of your own!!**

_____

_____

_____

_____

_____

Thankfully, I was able to recognize the hurt in me before I allowed it to totally affect my children. Often, the abused become the abusers, and even though my mindset was to not allow that, there was still some fallout from my childhood wounds. What I mean is that my pain therapy required I use all that negativity to fuel something positive. I began coaching my sons in youth sports. While I did not discipline the way that my stepfather did, I did and still do require a higher level of excellence from all three of my sons to this day.

It was important for me to go back and speak with my sons and talk about my issues and how they were affected. Make no mistake, to move forward successfully, you will need to go back and talk to the ones who you may have unintentionally hurt. I have seen this many times in ministry where we see powerful gifts in the body, but the children of such leaders will have nothing to do with them.

I get it. Sometimes being a "P.K." comes with certain expectations, but you mean to tell me that this word we are teaching is powerful enough to save others and their relationships, but our relationships with our own children are tattered and torn? This does not make any sense to me. We are teaching others how to reconcile with their families and children, but our own kids don't even want to talk to us? **This is a pattern in ministry that must not continue**! We must learn to apply the very lessons that we teach others to our own situations.

It may be frustrating, because usually as they get older they tend to give you less access to their lives if they have been hurt, so estrangement is simply a defense mechanism. Restoring your relationships with estranged children who have been hurt by <u>what you used to be</u> requires a specific set of actions to repair the breach:

## 1.) There Must Be Open And Honest Dialogue

- Be prepared to answer the tough questions honestly.

- You cannot forge a better relationship built on lies.
- Let them know the why to some of your behaviors.
- Be prepared for the backlash, it could be negative.

## 2.) <u>Own Your Mess</u>

- Acknowledge the hurts you have caused.
- Don't make excuses but offer insight.
- Seek first to understand before being understood.
- If you do not acknowledge them, you will lose them.

## 3.) <u>Don't Make Promises, Take Actions</u>

- Establish patterns of consistency.
- Don't just talk it, walk it! **<u>Show them they are more important than your title/ position/ministry!</u>**
- Look for nothing in return.
- It will take time, especially if they have been estranged for a while.

## 4.) <u>Remember They Are Older Now</u>

- They are not your babies anymore, and you must address them as peers, not as parents to children.

- Once they are older, they have the choice to make amends with you.
- Don't assume that since you seek to make amends that they will respond in similar fashion.
- It may take years of consistency, depending on how deep the wounds are.

## 5.) <u>Seek Family Counseling If Necessary</u>

- Family counseling is a fantastic way for everyone to express their feelings in the presence of a nonbiased third party.
- Involving/inviting them to your sessions will help them to heal as well.

# Chapter 10

# The Restored Image

*Time Does Not Make Great Leaders; God Does That*

The focus of this book has been about bringing light and understanding to the mental health crisis in the church. I believe getting back to the Ephesians 4 model of ministry will take away some of the burden of ministry for many leaders. We all have trouble balancing and maintaining life's simple priorities sometimes, and that's why we need help. This part might seem a little more preachy than the rest, but I assure you it's timed perfectly.

We are seeing an increase in the number of cases of mental/emotional cases in church leadership because God's plan for the body included the need for mental and emotional health as well. A greater understanding of the five-fold ministry mandate is needed within the leadership ranks of the body. The model was given to us for the purposes of not only maturing the body of Christ, but was also designed so that no one person bears the weight of an entire ministry by themselves. I don't know about you, but I don't want to be the only person in the room who hears from God. What a huge responsibility that is for any leader to always be the one "on game," as some of the younger generation might call it.

I hope you are beginning to see a pattern here. The leadership model listed in Ephesians chapter 4 is not describing some hierarchal leadership pattern for ministry, but a plurality of leadership that causes all people in the body to receive impartation from all the five-fold anointings. (1 Corinthians 12:28) speaks to the church governmental; responsibility of apostolic leadership, which is different from (Ephesians 4:11-13), which has to do with the **maturation** of the body. Let's review the text:

> "And God has appointed these in the church: **first apostles, secondly prophets, third teachers**, after that miracle and then gifts of healings, helps, administrations, varieties of tongues." (**1 Corinthians 12:28**) **NIV**

This scripture alludes to the apostles' governmental authority to establish a work. The other gifts assigned to an apostolic work are unable to function unless they are given a work to operate within. So, the hierarchal authority is only needed for direction and correction. This misunderstanding has caused the body of Christ to not be built up and matured in some of the most foundational areas, because they are usually receiving impartation from only one ministry gift. Typically, this leads to believers who are highly skilled in the same areas their leader is dominant in. By not properly understanding the five-fold ministry model, our deployment strategy has caused us to underutilize its potential.

**Let's look at the scripture in its entirety:**

> "And **He Himself gave** some to be **apostles, some prophets, some evangelist, and some pastors and teachers** [12] **for the equipping of the saints for the work of the ministry**, for the edifying of the body of Christ, [13] **Until we all come into the unity of the faith and of the knowledge of the son of God, to be a perfect man**, to the measure of the stature of the fullness of Christ." **(Ephesians 4:11-13)** NIV

Yeah, I know you have heard this scripture a thousand times before, but let's get some new revelation on the subject matter:

## 1.) <u>Christ Gave The Gifts To The Body (Vs. 11)</u>

- The gifts were given to serve the body.
- We always have a responsibility to teach no matter what team they play for.
- *Time does not make great leaders, God does that.*

## 2.) <u>Some Are Meant To Stay In The House To Teach (Vs. 11b)</u>

- Why are so many gifts away from the body? Where are all the ones He gave to "equip the saints for the work of the ministry"?
- Hierarchical type thinking does not allow for the expression of all five apostolic gifts, therefore the people are deprived of much needed impartation.
- **(The Hierarchical Model)** One office decides when/if the other gifts are "allowed" to speak to the people.
- **(The Plurality Model)** All gifts "share" the responsibility of leading and teaching equally. Therefore no one gets burned out. This is the reason you never saw a "board of directors" in the Bible.
- Many gifts are choosing to stay away because they have not been **put to proper use in the church**.

### 3.) <u>All Five Offices Have The Same Exact Job (Vs. 12)</u>

- "Equipping the saints to do the work of the ministry."
- This solidifies the plurality way of thinking.

### 4.) <u>The Job Does Not End Until We All Look Like Christ (Vs. 13)</u>

- If we are not there yet, then this model is still necessary.
- So, there are still apostles and prophets today!

I told you I was going to get a little preachy for a moment, but the goal was to bring a diverse set of spiritual eyes to focus on the word concerning God's structure for the church. Now what I am about to say is going to make some people mad, but as my aunt always says, "Nobody's mad but the devil!" Many have assigned the gifts God gave to the body to one gender more specifically than another: Male. After an extended study of the Father's heart for a sermon series, I began to understand a truth that was so plain it blew my mind. I had read the same scripture many times before, but I had never seen it like this. When we clear away our internal chatter, we can really hear what God is saying to us unencumbered.

## My Revelation at the Well

> "When a Samaritan woman came to draw water, Jesus said to her, "**Will you give me a drink?**" [8] (His disciples had gone into the town to buy food.) [9] The Samaritan woman said to him, "**You are a Jew, and I am a Samaritan woman. How can you ask me for a drink?**" (For Jews do not associate with Samaritans.) **(John 4:7-9)** NIV

The revelation the Holy Spirit dropped on me, that forever solidified my stance on women in ministry, is this: *A man who is thirsty does not care who gives him a drink of water!* They could be clean hands, dirty hands, black hands, white hands, male hands, or female hands, just give me something to drink! In other words, if they want Jesus, it does not matter the container it comes in, as long as it satisfies the need! Amen, somebody! Just because she began to "do the work of an evangelist" and told others about Christ doesn't mean all women are called to be evangelists in ministry. Many have been too caught up in the gender-specific roles of women in ministry and missed this important fact.

The men I can really depend on to walk along with me in ministry are strong individuals themselves, and the plurality ministry model is counterintuitive to the male nature. Sometimes we may feel that if we are not leading the charge then we are not making an impact, when nothing could be farther from the truth. So, working with someone who has a ministry that has already been birthed and needs that anointing they have is out of the question.

I recall an incident early on in ministry at Kingdom Empowerment Center. We had the opportunity to come together with two other young ministries that were experiencing some of the same challenges of ministry we were having. Each ministry had about thirty to fifty people. My stance was, *Let's come together. I don't care who leads it, I just want God to get the glory!* However, they both allowed their doors to close, and the sheep were scattered. I found it interesting that neither ever thought to send those individuals to us. The Bible says the "hireling cares nothing for the sheep." (John 10:13)

All of that to say this: I have found my gifted and anointed sisters are sometimes more faithful and capable than many of their male counterparts. There were times when I looked for a man, so I could just have a Sunday off, but I found none. Many years ago, my wife and I had decided to find a church home we both agreed on. We found ourselves at an AME church. The culture of the church was like many of the traditional denominational ministries. There were lots of liturgies and ceremonial regimen, including its stance on the charismatic gifts and women in ministry. In fact, I don't ever remember a teaching on the believers' spiritual giftings.

We had the opportunity to get to know and serve with a powerful woman of God, let's call her "Rev. Shirley Chisolm." This was the first time I had met a real prophet of God and she was not part of a charismatic church either, so her gifts were not even recognized. A member's daughter had gone missing, and she was distraught. Rev. Shirley told the family she saw where the daughter was, and that she and another girl had originally gone willingly with some men they met, but now they were being held against their will. She was able to give the police specific street markers in the area, which gave them a clue of where to start looking for the girls. So, you mean to tell me this powerful woman of God, gifted beyond any male preacher I had ever had the experience of knowing at that time, is disqualified from leading because she is a woman?

Rev. Shirley started a parachurch ministry on Saturdays and was effectively dismissed from her duties at the church. I believe in a similar situation, a man with the same anointing and gifts, would be hailed as a special gift to the body and would be allowed to continue leading in the ministry. I am happy to report the AME's stance on women in ministry has changed over the years. In 2000 **Vashti Murphy McKenzie** became the first female Presiding Bishop over the National AME Conference with a global membership of over 2.5

million church members. I loved the way she explained it in a 2019 Christian Post article I read, she said "Being able to get that message out, being able to show people that it's not just me being female, that I have had experiences, I'm qualified, and take a look at how God has blessed our ministry as an indication of what we can do in the future."

According to (Genesis 1:26-27), didn't God make male and female after His own image and likeness? So, explain to me why a woman can't effectively lead a ministry. Oh, I know it's because they are too emotional, right? Well guess what? Men are emotional too. Everybody is! We all have a unique way of expression when it comes to our emotions. Women may be more vocal about it, but men tend to be quiet, devious, and underhanded when challenged or wronged. So, who is the more qualified? That's not our job to decide. God never asked us to determine who was qualified for ministry, *that's His job*!

As a natural father, I would turn the world upside down to see the people I love and care about saved. Now, if I will do that as a natural father, how much more would our Father God use everything He has to bring His children to safety? You are correct, He would not spare anything! So, if a woman has a word in her mouth that will deliver my son, let her loose!

I believe once our focus in the church has been properly aligned with its real needs and issues, we will see the manifestation of the glorious church that the Bible talks about. Viewing the issues from the context of mental and emotional health, you will need every hand that is able. It won't even matter if they are male, female, young or old, just get me some help with all these broken people!

In closing, I know you are wondering whatever happened to my mother. Well, she got remarried to a wonderful man from Bermuda and they traveled the world. I realized I had never seen my mother truly happen until then. They had been married about fifteen years when he passed away from a heart attack. Several years later, my mother was diagnosed with a debilitating medical condition. For two years prior to her passing, she and I had the friendship I had always wanted.

She told me stories about my dad. For instance, I didn't know that at one time he had been a powerful young ministry gift himself. This brought so much clarity to me. I understood why my father was so angry when I would come home from going to church with my mom and tell him about Jesus. It seems that he had witnessed a young child get run over by a car, and his take on the matter was, "What kind of God would allow that to happen to an innocent child?" If you want to serve a God like that, you can go ahead, but I don't want to be a part of that!" It would seem this one incident had caused my dad to turn away from God.

When my mother passed away, she and I were best friends, and I was at peace. She left me with these words of wisdom: "When you know better, you do better." Someone asked me at the funeral why I wasn't more upset than I was. Why would I be upset about seeing a friend who had been suffering go home to be with the Lord?

Today, my wife and I serve as the founding pastors of Empowerment City Church, ATL, in McDonough, Georgia. We are established as an apostolic ministry plant to lay the groundwork for this next ministry shift from organization to organism. The Acts church must be apostolic in nature to affect not only geographical regions, but various world systems and sectors, such as government, business, entertainment, family, arts, media, and education. Over our twenty years in ministry, my wife and I have been foundational pastors of four church plants. We have mentored, supported many other startups, and established ministries alike with leadership training, financial support, equipment, and operational guidance where needed.

Our ultimate vision is the establishment of Empowerment University, the training and evangelistic arm of our ministry. **Empower-U** is a place where all believers can come for not just biblical training, but life skills training. I believe that we as the Body of Christ have been called to operate at a higher level in the society we live in. The body has never lacked people with the capacity to function at this level, but far too few ministries are training God's people with this level of understanding in mind. We at Empowerment City want to see the rise of the ministry of the believer in this age.

The final chapters of this book are still being written. I have learned to define what ministry success means for me, and today I am excited about all the possibilities that lie ahead.

Hello, my name is Michael Moses, and for the first time in my life, I know exactly what I am. I want you to know that I am okay with being:

***Blessed and Broken!***

CPSIA information can be obtained
at www.ICGtesting.com
Printed in the USA
LVHW071611220622
721699LV00019B/490